BICYCLING
COUNTRY
ROADS

BICYCLING COUNTRY ROADS

from
San Jose
to
Santa Barbara

Joanne Rife

Western Tanager Press
Santa Cruz

The material in this book is revised and updated at
each printing.
Cover design by Lynn Piquett
Photographs by the author

ISBN: 0-934136-16-5
Library of Congress Card Catalog Number: 81-52672

Printed in the United States of America

Western Tanager Press
1111 Pacific Ave.
Santa Cruz, CA 95060

To Ed
Through All The Years
and in memory of my father,
Austin I. Teasley
1909–1989
my first bicycling partner

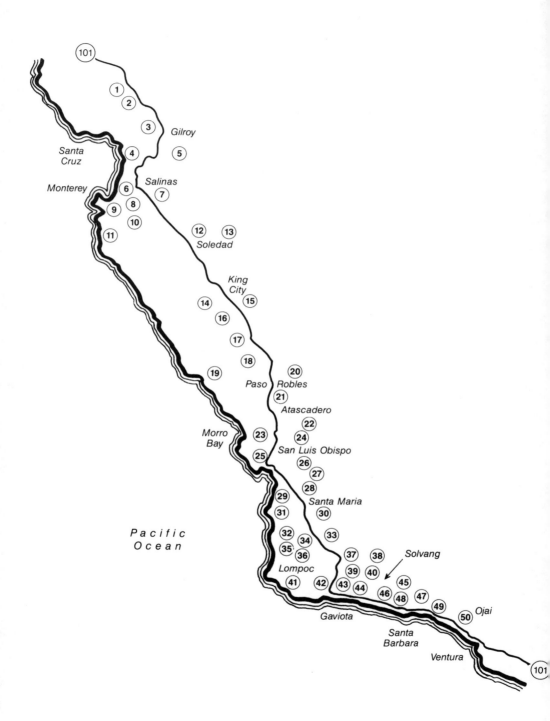

TABLE OF CONTENTS

INTRODUCTION

The Central Coast of California is an area still little discovered by the multitudes to the south and north. From Santa Barbara on the south to San Jose on the north, from the Pacific on the west, over the Coast Range to the valleys bordering Highway 101 and into the hills that stretch to the east is a land both tame and wild. The multitudes pass through occasionally, looking out their car windows and wondering what is beyond the margins of the freeway.

Plenty.

Increasing numbers have discovered the Central Coast as a place to live — not overcrowded, still blessed with unsullied air, yet not far from the big city life.

What the Central Coast is, for bicyclists, is near paradise: old country roads, lovely red-tiled missions, quiet canyons shaded by old oaks, pastel Victorians in little towns forgotten by time, the sparkle of sun off the ocean, dry rivers that lead to blue lakes. The southern half of the Central Coast is within three to four hours' drive of the Los Angeles area and the northern half in the same driving time from the Bay Area.

This book is designed to open new vistas for the many who have discovered the Central Coast and make their homes there, and for those urbanites looking for a weekend or a week of fine bicycling in a delightful new area. The rides are grouped for the most part so that those from out of the area can plan a weekend, or a week, for bicycling, using a base of operations. If the rides are too long or too difficult, many shortcuts or easy variations are noted. Conversely, if they are too easy, combinations can be put together to challenge the hardiest bicyclist. The rides vary from 10 miles to over 70. I think of them as 10-speed bicycle rides, although some can be accomplished without gears. I must say gearing equates with easier riding in my mind: all things become possible.

You might have noted I called the Central Coast a "near paradise." There is always some fly in the ointment. The fly, to me, is the wind. It can be circumvented, most often in fall and winter, and quite often in spring and summer, for it is usually an afternoon wind. It blows at least three quarters of the time from the west and the north and is liable to funnel up valleys that open to the sea: the Salinas, from Morro Bay, the Santa Maria, the Lompoc and Santa Ynez. It also blows down the coast, from north to south. Most of the trips try to make use of that wind with early starts going west and returning east.

All in all the weather is a blessing. The area is generally cooled by the influence of the Pacific, although it gets hot during July and August in the inland areas, including rides near King City, Paso Robles and Atascadero. The moderating influence of the sea means it also does not get cold in winter, again except in those inland areas.

Fog along the coast is another consideration, mostly because it will rob a day of its visual impact. It makes for pleasant bicycling temperatures, but I'll take the sun. The fog is mostly a creature of late spring and summer and burns off by noon.

The best cycling is in fall and spring. The area is glorious in spring, from about February through June. The winds begin to pick up by April and become a factor.

I have rated the rides, and the rating is very subjective. Some rides I would rate moderate one time out and difficult the next, so take the ratings with a grain of salt. Easy means flat. Moderate means flat with some hill work. Difficult means there is at least one hill that made me wish I were 1) younger, 2) in better condition, or 3) sedentary. Very difficult rides are exactly that. Just plain old hard, for one reason or another.

The points of interest I have talked about have a great deal to do with my interests: historical sites; restroom facilities; geological formations (hills in particular); on rides of over 30 miles, rough road surfaces; place names. I hope the information beyond the trip itself will enhance your ride.

The maps are not necessarily drawn to scale. The top of the page is north unless otherwise marked. Each map has a starting grid ⊠➔ to get you going in the right direction. Mileage figures are in parentheses. The information is current to 1981, although I have bicycled the region since 1965. Some parts I know better than others — from Santa Barbara to San Luis Obispo; and around the Morgan Hill-Gilroy and Monterey area. Others I am still discovering and exploring.

I wish this were the kind of book in which I could prattle on about my adventures: the baby gopher snake in the road that had the temerity to coil up and strike at me when I was only trying to be friendly; when the crotch in my shorts gave way; oranges eaten beside the road under old oaks; the mistake of onions in sandwiches and chocolate bars for desert; getting quickly back on the bike when hearing a car laboring up a hill behind me — no need anyone else knowing I was off and walking.

What more is there to say? If you are reading this you already know bicycling is the best way to maneuver over a road, providing the road is worth maneuvering over.

That is what is so marvelous about the Central Coast — its roads are worth maneuvering over.

Enjoy!

Morgan Hill, 1982

The last unsold copies of the 1982 version of *Bicycling Country Roads* were destroyed in the 1989 Loma Prieta Earthquake, mushed in their cartons when Western Tanager's warehouse in Santa Cruz crumpled. Some books go out with a whimper and others with a bang.

On the plus side, it was time for the book to be updated. Once I was out on the road doing the update I was stunned by the changes that had occurred over the past decade. In order to get the work done as quickly as possible, I drove over every road in my trusty Honda, wishing time and again I could be riding my trusty Trek.

This is one beautiful state. The increase in population is apparent, however. Every road except those in the farthest reaches carries more cars, and there are certainly more houses and more construction. Some attractions are gone (the Diablo Canyon Nuclear Energy Information Center) and others added (the Monterey Bay Aquarium). Some roads are in far better condition, others far worse.

The most important change in bicycling in the past decade is the emphasis on safety, particularly the use of helmets. Wear them, and use a rearview mirror. Be alert, use your ears and use your eyes.

Bicycling can be dangerous. I know. On August 24, 1989, my father was killed while riding his bicycle along a shoulderless state highway near Klamath. A logging truck passed but cut in too soon. My father was killed instantly. The trucker, originally charged in Del Norte County with hit-and-run, never spent a day in jail. California needs better roads, tougher laws and stronger sentences to protect bicyclists and pedestrians. For too long roads have been built as though the only thing that needs to go from point A to point B is a motor vehicle. Often there is no place to ride safely and no place to walk safely along major and minor thoroughfares.

Bicycle riders need to protect themselves now and lobby for the future. Helmets and political clout are weapons. Use them both.

Morgan Hill, 1990

1 CALERO LAKE

Distance: *18 miles*
Loop
Traffic: *light*
Rating: *easy to moderate*
Side trip: *12 miles, easy*

A lake speckled with speedboats and waterskiers is the focus of this 18-mile ride just north of Morgan Hill. A good place to park your car is the lot for County Transit patrons at Tilton and Hale avenues in Morgan Hill. Take the Cochrane off-ramp from Highway 101, proceed west to Monterey Highway, turn right to Tilton and left to Hale. The lot is on the left.

Once on your bicycle, head north on Hale Avenue 0.3 mile to Willow Springs Road, and turn left, heading up Willow Springs Canyon. Fields of oats and old oak trees border the winding country road that after half a mile starts uphill to cross a saddle before dropping down to Chesbro Lake. The steep uphill is less than a mile and the only substantial climb on the entire route, but is a bit of a huffer and puffer. Soon, however, you are across the top and down the other side, past several private rural paradises to the intersection with Oak Glen Avenue (2.9). A right turn and you will have Chesbro Lake on your left. Fish

abound in this small lake in a quiet valley. On the right, houses cling to the hillside, hoping to keep from landing on your handlebars. Beer and wine are available at the Quail Canyon Inn beside the lake.

At the upper end of the lake the junction to Calero Lake appears (4.5). Turn right on Uvas Road (G8) and begin a gradual uphill pull with Uvas Creek flowing along the right. Extensive equine facilities are located in the valley, which widens slowly. Cattle, the spreading California oak, and picturesque old barns dot the rolling hills.

Uvas Road turns into McLean Road and begins to climb over a saddle in the hills. Lovely large homes are tucked into the mountain folds and sit along the ridge lines. After gaining the top, a swift ride down the hill and into the broad valley that contains Calero Lake will bring you by Bailey Avenue (8.9). Bailey is the way out, but for now pedal by it a mile and go down to Calero Lake County Park, where there are swimming, picnicking and restroom facilities. Motorboats and jet-skis ply this lake, with an occasional sailboat gliding by if the wind is up. On warm summer days there is always much to watch. Just past the entrance to the park, on

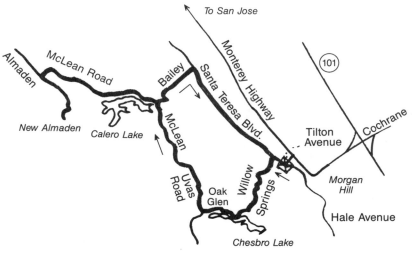

the right, is the Calero Inn, where lunches and refreshments are available.

Return to Bailey Avenue and turn left, toward the east (10.5). After a short climb there is a rollicking one-mile descent over very rough pavement. Out in the flat of the South Santa Clara Valley, in the middle of a most rural scene, is the large IBM complex, with four-lane roads and heavy traffic at quitting time. Past IBM, turn right at Santa Teresa Boulevard (12.8). It will be flat and spinning time all the way home. The shoulders on Santa Teresa are made for bicyclists. The area is still agricultural, with many orchards and vegetable fields. Just past San Bruno Avenue is a small strawberry stand on the right. In season, there are the most scrumptious strawberries, and with just a mile or two to go, it would be worth chancing strawberry jam to get them back to the car. Also down the road is a mushroom farm where mushrooms may be purchased.

Just a mile more completes a trip that has swung by two lakes, rural scenery, a huge electronics plant, and strawberries.

SIDE TRIP: *12 miles*

NEW ALMADEN

Continuing north on McLean through an ever-widening and flat valley, the traffic count will pick up and the road widen as civilization nears. Watch on the right for a large barn and dried fruit stand if you want to load your bicycle with goodies. About three miles down the road McLean turns sharply left at the juncture with Harry Road. Turn left and continue on to the intersection with Almaden Road and turn left again. The ride into New Almaden moves easily up the narrowing valley and finally narrowing road into the tiny town, which bills itself as California's first mining town. Settled in the mid-1800s after the founding of New Almaden Quicksilver Mine, the little town seems crammed down in the bottom of a steep-sided canyon. There are several restaurants, and a look at the Opry House and restaurant, on the left, is fun. The Opry House is the old Casa Grande, built in 1854 and a focus of much social life in the early days. The town museum is also interesting. It is on the left in the Carson House. Returning the way you came puts you back at Calero Lake.

2 TWO LAKES LOOP

Distance: *16 miles*
Loop
Traffic: *light*
Rating: *easy to moderate*
Side trip: *9 miles, moderate*

Blue lakes, white sails, country roads bordered with old oaks, tiny farms, and new homes combine to make the Uvas-Chesbro lakes loop a varied and delightful ride.

A good starting point is at the intersection of Edmundson and Oak Glen, west of Morgan Hill. (To get there turn west off Monterey Street in south Morgan Hill at Edmundson Avenue.) Head south down Oak Glen with Llagas Creek on the left and new ranch-style homes on the right. The road winds past old oaks and little farms and orchards to Sycamore Avenue (0.9). A turn to the right will send you around a hill and across a small valley and up a short, one-third-of-a-mile hill to cross a ridge with a pleasant ride down the other

side, past sheep and chickens and cows to Watsonville Road (2.9). Make a right turn and watch for heavier traffic for a half mile until a right turn onto Uvas Road (3.4). On the left is a pleasant winery, Sycamore Creek, where a pause may be made to check out the local wines. On this trip you will be able to buy wine, stained glass windows and custom dog houses. Strapping them to the back of the bicycle may be a problem.

At Uvas Lake (5.8) weekends are especially pleasant, with the lake full of sailboats and windsurfers. It is a popular spot for catamarans; and when a pleasant breeze is blowing, the fleet boats will be zipping back and forth, their skippers hung out over the hull and crew hanging from a trapeze, trying to keep on the brink of disaster at all times. Those who go over provide moments of interest as the wet sailors pull them back upright. There are picnic tables and restroom facilities at the little park.

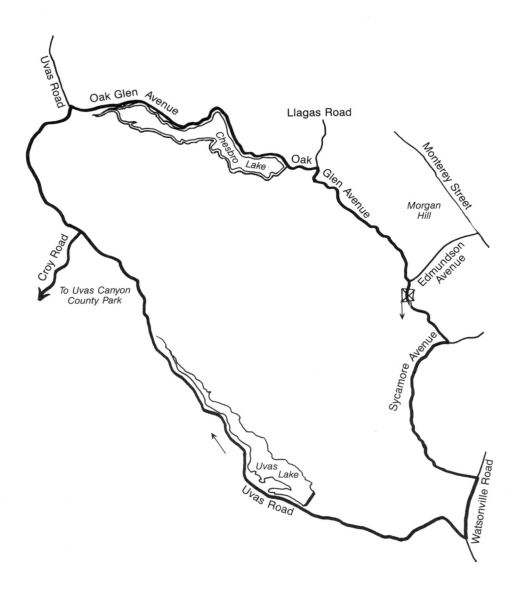

Uvas Road

Oak Glen Avenue

Llagas Road

Monterey Street

Chesbro Lake

Oak Glen Avenue

Morgan Hill

Croy Road

To Uvas Canyon County Park

Edmundson Avenue

Sycamore Avenue

Uvas Lake

Watsonville Road

Uvas Road

The lake is about two miles long, following the creek bed as it winds up Uvas Canyon. Beyond the lake there are several large ranches and the country opens out some. Once over the narrow bridge and up the ridge you are at the highest elevation on the ride, and it is more or less all downhill from here.

The road slides on through the rolling hills dotted with cattle and down a quick descent to the junction at Oak Glen Avenue (11.0). Go right; quickly Chesbro Lake hoves into view ahead. Beer, wine, and fishing tales are available at Quail Canyon Inn (no fights allowed, reads the sign). Chesbro may have a few sailboats, but fishermen like it best; at least the fishermen gulls think it contains enough fish to make good eating.

Past the dam and down the hill is the junction with Llagas Road (14.1). Turn right for a lovely two-mile ride, still on Oak Glen Avenue, back to Edmundson. The road winds comfortably downward with Llagas Creek on the left and smells as intoxicating as a bakery.

A fine conclusion for the ride would be a quick left turn at Edmundson to Richert and Sons Winery, just a tenth of a mile, to test the fine wines in the cool building.

SIDE TRIP: *9 miles*

UVAS CANYON COUNTY PARK

A left turn at Croy Road will send you off toward Uvas Canyon County Park. The road dips and climbs upward for four and a half miles through a steadily narrowing canyon that soon takes on the look of a mountain setting. A quiet creek slides along on the right, digger pines and redwoods press in on both sides, little mountain cabins teeter on the abyss. Suddenly the road narrows to one lane at a gate to Sveadal, a private resort. Continue through the gate. Tennis courts, a pool and small cabins line the road. Pedal up a final grade and you are at the park. Overnight camping, hiking, and picnicking are available in a setting shaded by madrone trees, redwoods and oaks. It is cool in the shade and the bright moss glows in the filtered sunlight. And just think, it is all downhill back to Uvas Road.

3 WINERY ROW

Distance: *11 miles*
Loop
Traffic: *light to moderate*
Rating: *easy*
Side trip: *10 miles, easy*

This is a bicycle trip that will include the small premium wineries of the Uvas Valley and Hecker Pass, rural scenes, and, with a side trip, a bit of small-town flavor.

Start at the intersection of Day Road and Santa Teresa Boulevard. (To reach the area, turn west off Highway 101 at Masten Avenue, north of Gilroy, and turn south on Monterey Street to Day Road, turn west about three quarters of a mile and park.)

Day Road jogs to the right. Take the jog right and left, heading west into the hills, past large farms, fields of oats, rambling farm houses. The flat South Santa Clara Valley gives way to the beginning of small rolling hills. At certain times of the year the seasoned smells of the Gilroy area's famous crop, garlic, liberally laced with onion, will spice your way. One can hardly wait for a good red wine and a bowl of spaghetti to go with the aroma.

Begin the easy climb past large new homes encroaching on the fields. The road makes a sharp left and right as it heads into the hills. There is a home development here tucked back in the folds, one of those popular retreats from city life that are found throughout the state. Harbingers of what lies ahead appear on the right — vineyards in their various seasonal hues. Down the easy grade past the vineyards, grazing cattle, and a small reservoir is the Watsonville Road (3.4).

Turn right, north, for a quick visit to Kirigin Cellars, our first winery. It stands on the site of the historic Solis Rancho homestead, and wines are made from grapes grown primarily on the 50-acre estate. It is open daily. Return to Watsonville Road and head south. Traffic is somewhat heavier and shoulders are piecemeal, but there should be no problem. Watch for a huge, old weathered barn on the left. Continue

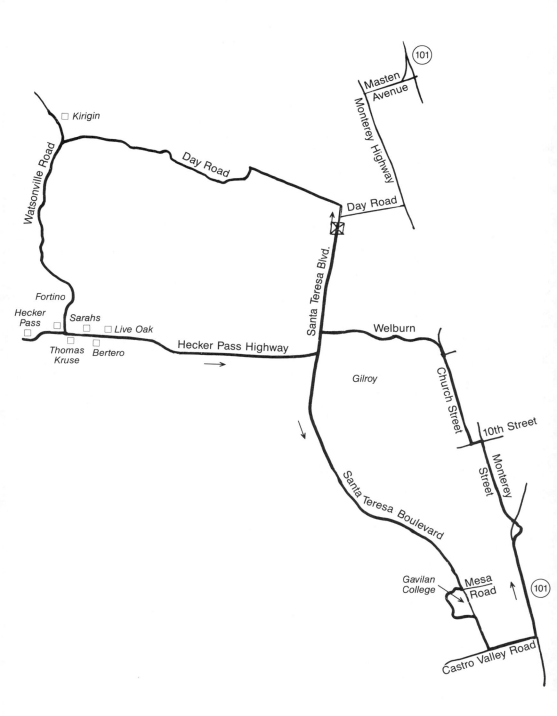

GAVILAN COLLEGE AND GILROY

An opportunity to see the Gavilan College Campus, a community college serving the Gilroy-Hollister-Morgan Hill area, and to visit Gilroy and its museum may be taken with a right turn, south, on Santa Teresa Boulevard. There are wide shoulders and a marked bike trail to speed your way. After an easy climb along the base of the hills, a right turn at Mesa Road after about four miles will take you onto the campus. The student union, the large building on the left just past the flagpole, offers food and drink when school is in session. A quick spin under the footbridge and past the duck pond will put you back on Santa Teresa. Continue right, to Castro Valley Road, and turn left to Monterey Highway (101). Fruit stands on the right and across the highway are an excellent source of vitamins. Cherries, plums, oranges, pears — whatever is in season — are available. Cross the highway carefully (there is a median to ease your way) and then proceed left (north) toward Gilroy. You will be on the highway only one mile. Take the first off-ramp, Monterey Street, go under the freeway and pedal about two miles to Tenth Street, the first signal. Turn left, go two blocks, and turn right on Church Street. This pleasant, wide boulevard leads through an older section of town. On the corner of Fifth and Church streets is the Gilroy Museum, in the old Carnegie Library building, open daily except Tuesdays and Sundays. Proceed past First Street and turn left on Welburn to Santa Teresa. A right turn returns you to the beginning at Day Road.

on past Adams Picnic Site on the right to the intersection at Hecker Pass Road (5.8). Take a right turn for a short visit to two wineries. The first is Fortino Winery, where the wines show three generations of wine-making skill. It is also open daily, as is the next winery, Hecker Pass, where other members of the Fortino family hold sway. After a visit in the tasting room, turn around and head due east on Hecker Pass Highway. Just past the Watsonville Road, on the right, is the Thomas Kruse Winery, which specializes in fine dry table wines and some champagne. Founded in 1971, the winery has gained substantial notoriety for its product. Also on the right you will see a cactus farm, where the Mexican spice *nopales* is grown.

Continuing down Hecker Pass, on the left is a small winery, Sarah's Vineyards, established in 1978. The tasting room is open by appointment only. The next winery in line is Solis Winery, on the right, founded in 1917. In addition to wines it grows the largest California live oak in the country. On the left is Live Oak Winery. Peter Scagliotti is the wine maker and it too is open daily. Farther along the road is Hecker Pass Family Adventure with a picnic area and rides. There is an admission fee. A flower seed farm brightens the way.

If you can still balance on the bicycle, continue on into Gilroy to the signal at Santa Teresa Boulevard (9.1).

Turn north for a ride back to the car (11.3).

4 RIO DEL MAR AND ENVIRONS

Distance: *23 miles*
Loop
Traffic: *light to heavy*
Rating: *moderate to difficult*

There are a couple of hills that might make a believer out of one's thigh muscles at the end of this beach-residential-industrial-rural ride that is filled with variety. It begins at the Highway 1 off-ramp at Rio del Mar Boulevard, six miles east of Santa Cruz. Parking is available at Deer Park Shopping Mall west of the highway.

and wind through an open valley toward the beach. Just under the railroad bridge is the turn into Manresa State Beach (5.2). The bluff above the beach is a favorite spot for watching the gray whale migration in summer and winter. January and February are particularly good months. The 40- to 60-foot behemoths can be seen with binoculars; the spray when they blow can be seen with the naked eye. When the whales are not migrating, surfers riding the combers below are the other interesting fauna to watch.

Take Rio del Mar west toward the beach, up over the hill, through a residential area. Turn left at Sumner Avenue (0.6). The road speeds downward with eucalyptus and cypress shading the pavement on one side and pleasant homes on the other. The Seascape Golf Course drops down beside the road. At Seascape Boulevard (2.3) turn left through a neighborhood. At San Andreas Road (3.2), turn right

The road continues along just inside the first row of low hills from the sea bluffs, but glimpses of the ocean can be caught through the trees. The entrance to Sunset Beach, one of the premier beaches along Monterey Bay, is at 7.6 miles. It is less than a mile down to the beach and the road runs along the dunes for another mile and a half before you must backtrack to San Andreas. Continue on through rolling hills, heav-

ily farmed, down into the Pajaro Valley. Turn left on Beach Road (9.6) and ride under the freeway and into Watsonville.

Watsonville was founded in 1852 by Judge John H. Watson. Its first hotel was a tent, and its principal crop was potatoes. In 1853, however, apple trees were planted, and the area became famed for its apples. It is still a major farming community. The road takes you through a warehouse, packing shed and cold storage area. Turn left on Walker Street (12.2), bumping over railroad tracks, past canning companies, frozen food producers, chemical companies, steel companies and then, whisk, out of town across Harkins Slough and past Ramsay Park, where steel gives way to tennis rackets, then cattle.

Walker Street becomes Harkins Slough Road. The road is very narrow. Turn right at Green Valley Road (13.6)

and left on Highway 152, Main Street (14.8). At Holm Road, turn right, then immediately left onto Westgate Drive, a frontage road to Highway 1. Go straight across Airport Boulevard (16.8). You are now on Larkin Valley Road. The area is surprisingly settled — a mixture of old (small) and new (big) houses. Horses, sheep and cattle graze in the pretty valleys.

The road climbs up out of the valley, putting the bicycle in lower gears. Larkin Valley empties suddenly onto the freeway (22.0), or under the freeway. Slip under, then turn right on Bonita Road and climb back to cross the freeway again at Freedom Boulevard. Turn left onto Soquel Drive. After paralleling the freeway, turn left on Rio del Mar Boulevard and cross over the freeway for the last time to Deer Park (23.0).

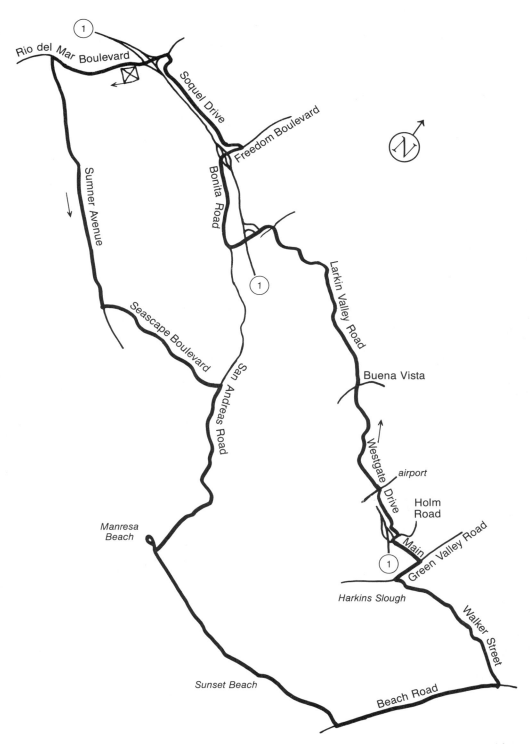

11

5 HOLLISTER AND SAN JUAN BAUTISTA

Distance: *20 miles*
Loop
Traffic: *light to moderate*
Rating: *easy*

Two old western towns, one very American, the other very Spanish, are the focus of this ride in San Benito County. Hollister's old buildings have the look of the old west and several Victorian homes from the last century sit beside its streets. San Juan Bautista's focal point is the old Spanish mission and its several adobes dating from the mid-1800s.

We will start in Hollister, an easy drive from Highway 101 on Highway 25, south of Gilroy. Hollister is a town of about 18,000, founded in 1862, and has several motels. There are a number of bicycling trips from the Hollister area that might be tried over a weekend.

Our journey begins at the corner of Fourth (Highway 156) and West streets, two blocks west of the main intersection ((Highways 156 and 25). Just south of the corner at West and Ann is the San Benito County Historical Society Museum, which is open on Saturdays and Sundays and gives a glimpse into the background of this small county. Proceeding south on West Street, you might want to wander along several streets in this older part of town, for there are old homes of interest, particularly on Fifth Street. At Nash Road (0.8), turn right to go out of town, crossing the San Benito River to Riverside Road (1.9) and turning left. Sheep, horses, orchards, red-tailed hawks will fill your field of vision. At the intersection with Union Road, turn right. The country opens out and a marked shoulder will speed you on your way, past the sudden industrial complex of Teledyne McCormick Selph tucked in the hills, to Highway 156 (5.1) and the fertile San Juan Valley.

Cross the highway and bear right to Mitchell Road. At Freitas Road (5.5),

turn left. Sweeping views are on either side, ahead and behind, with the Hollister Hills and Gabilan Peak (3,169) on the left, and the Flint Hills on the right. Receding behind is the Diablo Range. At Bixby Road (7.4) turn right. A variety of crops is grown in the San Juan Valley. Apricots, lettuce, spinach, broccoli and cauliflower are among the fruits and vegetables raised. Turn left on Duncan Road, right on Lucy Brown Lane (8.9) and left on San Justo Road. There is a gladness about the land, its reach, its openness, that makes for a

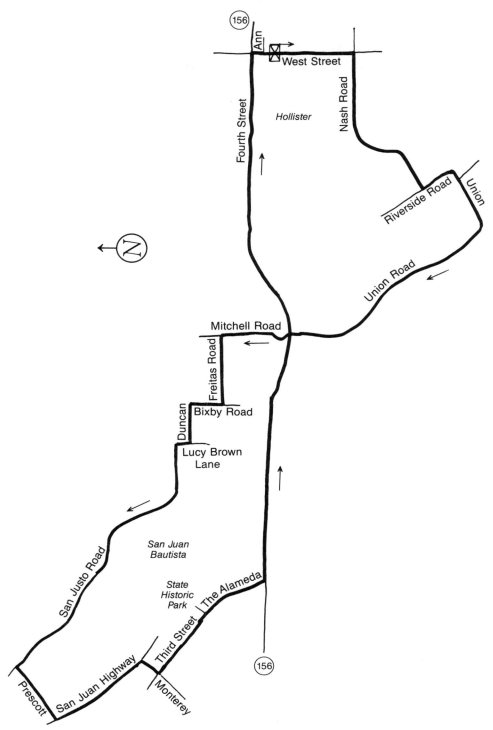

156

Ann

West Street

Fourth Street

Hollister

Nash Road

Riverside Road

Union

Union Road

N

Mitchell Road

Freitas Road

Bixby Road

Duncan

Lucy Brown Lane

San Justo Road

San Juan Bautista

State Historic Park

The Alameda

Third Street

156

San Justo Road

San Juan Highway

Monterey

Prescott

13

sense of freedom. A left on Prescott Road (10.7) and another left on San Juan Highway (11.2) will bring you to San Juan Bautista. A right turn on Monterey Street and left on Third Street will place you directly in the middle of town.

With a population of about 1,650, San Juan remains an unspoiled delight. Restaurants, boutiques and antique stores line the main street. Lock up your bike and take a walking tour. Brochures are available at the bakery at Polk Street and Third, where a wire stand is called the Chamber of Commerce. If you can escape the bakery without buying something, led by your nose, you are a better man or woman than I.

Undoubtedly the most interesting aspect of San Juan is the State Historic Park (Second and Washington streets),

with its fine restored buildings around the town square. The stately mission, founded in 1797, made it through the 1906 earthquake, which, with the ensuing fire, destroyed San Francisco. Yet it sits cheek by jowl to the San Andreas fault. The escarpment of the fault runs just north of the mission. Be sure to visit the seismograph display just east of the mission.

Third Street becomes Alameda and intersects with Highway 156 (12.6). Turn left on 156 and head for Hollister. The two-lane highway has broad shoulders most of the way. The moderate traffic moves quickly. In the afternoon a helpful tail wind may blow you back to your car. Once back in Hollister a turn right on West (19.8) will return you to your gas guzzler.

6 STRAWBERRY FIELDS FOREVER

Distance: *30 miles*
Loop
Traffic: *light to moderate*
Rating: *moderate*

The Pajaro River starts at San Felipe Lake and flows down to the sea between Sunset Beach and Zmudowski Beach in Monterey Bay. The word *pajaro* in Spanish means bird, but historically it has been used to mean border. It is the border between Santa Clara and San Benito counties and between Santa Cruz and Monterey counties. It also formed the boundary between several Spanish land grant ranchos. It is a winding, rather pleasant stream, bordered for our purposes by Highway 129.

Our ride starts just west of Highway 101 on 129 and heads west through the canyon. For a good part of the 129 ride, there will be a wide shoulder, although it narrows occasionally. Traffic is light to moderate. Small farms and homes

are scattered along the way, hidden in oaks and cottonwoods. At River Oaks (1.9) there is a small store and a cluster of houses. Go under the railroad bridge and up the other side, and soon, on the left, can be seen a large rock and gravel pit that has been burrowed a bleak half mile into the hills. There are a number of quarries in the area, which produces construction material of good quality.

The country opens out onto the coastal shelf that borders Monterey Bay. This is the Pajaro Valley, famous for its strawberry fields. Also farmed are artichokes, cauliflower, apples and other berries. The road straightens and comes into Watsonville. At the signal at the intersection of Highway 129 (Riverside Drive) and G12 (Main Street), turn left to Pajaro (12.2), and left again after crossing the river at the signal on San Juan Road (G11). Out of town the deep chocolate-brown soil indicates the fertile loam that has made this area one of

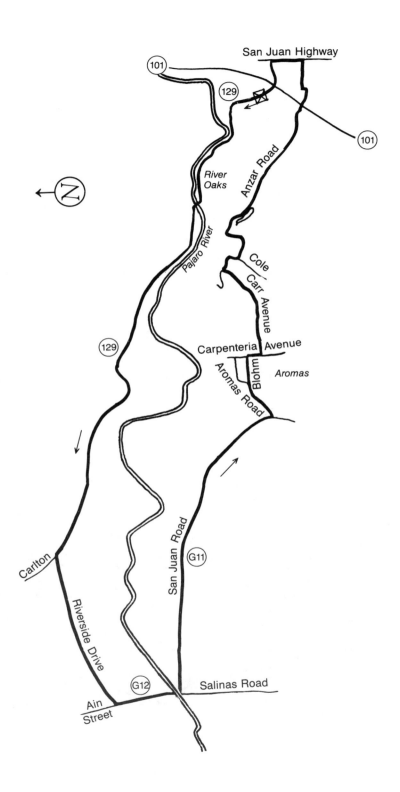

San Juan Highway

101

129

101

River
Oaks

Anzar Road

Pajaro River

Cole

Carr Avenue

129

Carpenteria Avenue

Aromas

Blohm

Aromas Road

San Juan Road

G11

Carlton

Riverside Drive

G12

Ain
Street

Salinas Road

N

the best for farming in the state. The road is flat. As it swings south, a rather intimidating hill looms ahead. It is just as high as it looks; however, no higher. At the top make a left turn onto Aromas Road (17.9) and pass the Christmas tree farms. As Aromas swings left, turn right on Blohm Avenue and go into the tiny town of Aromas. There is a small store at the corner of Aromas and Carpenteria Road, and a Mexican restaurant, where refreshments may be obtained. Turn right on Carpenteria and head up the hill to Carr Avenue and turn left (20.8). Carr is easy to miss. It is a narrow road about half way up the hill. There will be a mile and a half of hill work on Carr as the road climbs up to a saddle past a number of houses and small acreages hidden from the hurly-burly of the outside world. Once at the top, however, it is all downhill.

On the way down, Carr joins Anzar Road. Do not miss the abrupt turn-off, to the left, of Anzar Road (23.4). It drops down across a little valley and into a cool eucalyptus grove. Down goes the road through quiet valleys and across rolling hills. Anzar Lake boasts coots and ducks sporting in the water. Fresh brown eggs are for sale at one small farm. Cattle browse the hillsides. The narrow road rolls by old barns and slips under the freeway by a trailer park and comes out in the San Juan Valley at San Juan Highway (27.1). Turn left and ride to the Highway 129 intersection (28.3) where another left turn to cross over the freeway brings one back to the starting point (29.6).

7 SALINAS VALLEY AND STEINBECK

Distance: *28 miles*
Loop
Traffic: *light to moderate*
Rating: *easy*

The Salinas Valley is called the Salad Bowl of the Nation. With good reason. This ride along the Salinas River and through the middle of the Valley, culminating in Salinas at John Steinbeck's beautifully restored house, will give ample evidence that the name is true. Steinbeck, a Pulitzer Prize and Nobel Prize winner for literature, was a hometown boy. Severa. of his short stories and novels are set in the area, most particularly *East of Eden*.

I recommend a morning ride, for the winds can be very bothersome, particularly in the afternoon. Access to the starting point is the Highway 68 off-ramp from Highway 101 at John Street in Salinas. Starting at the corner of John and Main streets (Highway 68), head south. The wide four-lane street is a busy city thoroughfare, but within a mile you will be out of town. The town's population is 102,000. It was founded in 1852 and was a stage stop between San Juan Bautista and Monterey. Later it prospered as an agricultural center.

The Valley is flat and has become more so with agricultural use. Swinging out of town, get off the highway at River Road (3.4), taking a right off-ramp and progressing left under the highway on G17. The area is particularly beautiful in spring with the green mountains as a backdrop to the crops. The dark, sandy loam soil gives every indication of what it is capable of producing. When you see a sign on the right, Las Palmas Ranch, look to the right at a huge Victorian mansion, built in 1891.

The road wanders along the base of the hills, sometimes close to the Salinas River, sometimes not. Along the foothills are new residential areas. The road climbs up some gentle spurs from the Santa Lucia Mountains and down again. The tiny community of Buena Vista is named after the ranchos Buena Vista and Llano de Buena Vista, granted to the Estrada family in 1822 and 1823. The old schoolhouse is now the Grange.

At the Chualar River Road (12.7), turn left across the one-lane green girder bridge and pedal across the pastoral Valley. At the stop sign, turn left to follow Chualar River Road (14.8), and right, across the 101 freeway, into the town of Chualar. With a population of 400, Chualar rests on a site of a Spanish land grant. It was founded in 1874. Continue straight ahead on Main Street to Lincoln, turn left and then right on Chualar Road (15.5). Heading east across the Salinas Valley, turn left at Old Stage Road (16.8). As you pedal northward, the Gabilan range is on the right and the Santa Lucia Mountains on the left. Fields of lettuce, artichokes, celery, beans, cauliflower, peppers, sugar beets, depending on the season, line each side of the road.

Eucalyptus windbreaks march toward the hills. Some farming has gone indoors, in large greenhouse complexes. Bear to the left at Encinal. At the intersection at Old Stage Road and Alisal, take Alisal straight ahead (21.0). As you pedal toward town past the Salinas Municipal Airport, the flatness breaks up. Bear left at the elementary school, continuing on Alisal. Entering Salinas, the town will grow progressively older as you near the core. Go under the 101 freeway and under the railroad bridge, and turn right on Main Street (28.3) to find the Salinas restoration and revitalization project, bringing new life to the old downtown.

Turn left on Central Avenue (28.6). At the corner of Lincoln and Central is Austin House, built in 1896; at Stone and Central, the Steinbeck House, built in 1892. Both are restored. The Steinbeck House was the author's birthplace and is now a tearoom serving

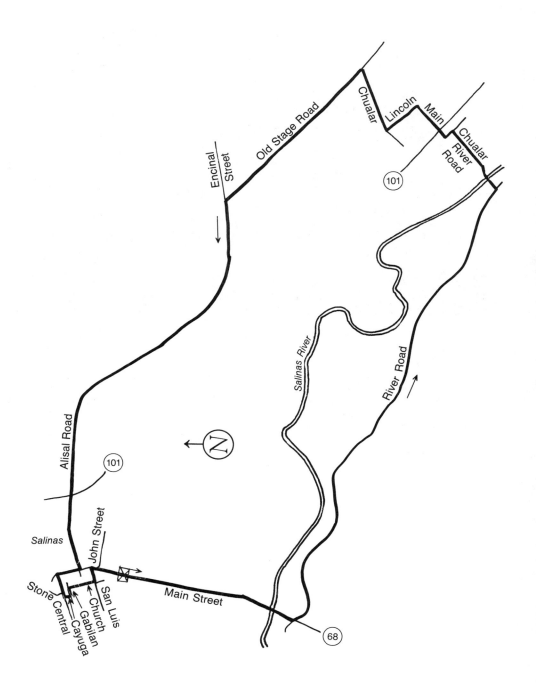

luncheon Monday through Friday. Reservations are required (408-424-2735). Two other restored homes are in the same block—the Mayer House, 1890, and the Krough House, 1900.

Turn left on Cayuga Street, where another restoration is on the left, the Empire House, 1892, and pedal to the Monterey County Court House, turn left on Gabilan Street and right on Church Street to San Luis Street, where you turn left again. The Steinbeck Library is on the left, where the author did much of his research for *East of Eden*. The Steinbeck Room has memorabilia, first editions and original manuscripts. The bronze statue of the author is in front of the library. A right turn to Main Street and back to John Street (28.1) brings the pedaler home.

8 PAJARO VALLEY BIRD WATCH

Distance: *23 miles*
Loop
Traffic: *light to moderate*
Rating: *easy to moderate*

The open Pajaro Valley, the rolling dunes of Elkhorn Slough, and a lovely county park are all part of this ride through the canyons and valleys of northern Monterey County.

The trip starts in Pajaro (which means bird in Spanish) at the intersection of G11 and G12 (San Juan and Salinas roads). It can be reached off Highway 129 just east of Highway 1 (Riverside Drive off-ramp) or west of Highway 101. Turn south off 129 to reach Pajaro. Take binoculars along for bird watching.

Aboard the bicycle, head south through Pajaro's commercial district. At the Y take Elkhorn Road (1.5) left, avoiding a hill. Elkhorn turns right in one mile at an intersection with Hall Road. Keep on Elkhorn through open country. Within another mile you will be at the first branch of the horn. Horses stand ankle deep in the incoming tide, and cattle graze the hills along the side of the slough. At Kirby Park Access Area

(4.8) you can pedal down to the slough and along the fishing roads that lead from Kirby. Many water fowl enjoy the slough — grebes, coots, migrating ducks, geese, egrets, herons. Back on Elkhorn, you drop down and across the slough at one point and then move uphill into a eucalyptus grove where sunlight dapples the road. Huge coastal live oaks tower over one's head. Elkhorn Slough National Estuarine Sanctuary is a "must see" stop (7.6).

The road slips down through scattered homes and intersects with Castroville Boulevard (9.3). Turn left and pedal along a pleasant, wide two-lane road that climbs slowly upward and then turns down to San Miguel Canyon Road (12.2). Moderate traffic count occurs along this artery (G12), but there is a wide shoulder. Just past the Pond Derosa turn right on Echo Valley Road (13.2). The hanging valley has sides, and up the side we go on Maher Road (13.6) with a left turn at the school.

Royal Oaks Park is beyond the steep little hill with its delicious swoop down the other side. Turn into the park (14.7) for a picnic lunch, restroom facilities,

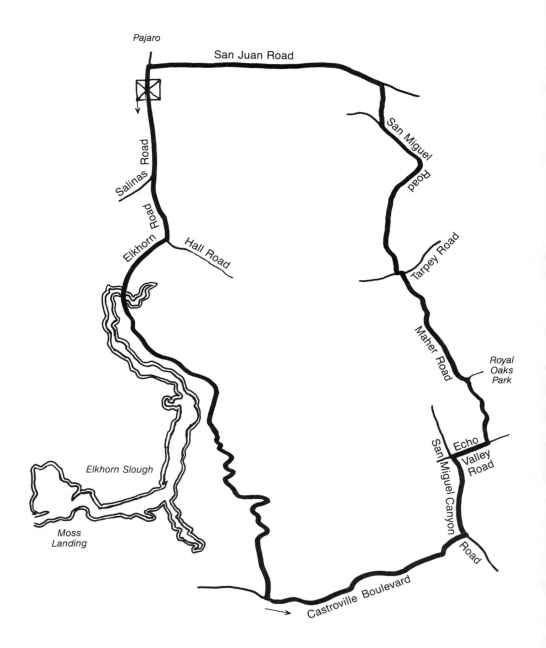

Pajaro

San Juan Road

San Miguel Road

Salinas Road

Elkhorn Road

Hall Road

Tarpey Road

Maher Road

Royal Oaks Park

Echo Valley Road

San Miguel Canyon Road

Elkhorn Slough

Moss Landing

Castroville Boulevard

slides, tennis courts, swings and things. This is a lovely park, very well-maintained and a joy to enjoy. The road continues down a pretty canyon with something unusual around every bend, at the bottom of every hill. There are a number of homes, both new and old, well-maintained and ramshackle.

Dropping out of the hills you come to Tarpey Road (16.5). Jog left and right onto San Miguel Canyon Road again, this time much reduced in size. Up hills and down there are many little reservoirs during the rainy months where fugitives from the slough bask in the warm winter sun. The road drops down into the Pajaro Valley and intersects with San Juan Road (19.6). Turn left and ride through the strawberry fields. Field workers keep each of the millions of plants under control: stooping, bending, chopping, picking, as the seasons run past.

Pajaro is a city of 1,500, with many cold storage and packing houses. The area grows broccoli, cabbage, lettuce, and many row crops. Once into Pajaro you will pedal about a mile back to the start (22.9).

9 MONTEREY PENINSULA

Distance: *23 miles*
Loop
Traffic: *moderate to heavy*
Rating: *easy to moderate*
Cutoff: *4 miles*

The Monterey Peninsula is one of the stellar bicycling areas in California. If you can catch it on a clear day, which is easier in fall and winter than in spring and summer, it is a total joy. On foggy days it retains an aura of mystery, but even then the fog usually burns away by midday. There are many rides in the area, including the historical route marked on the streets of Monterey. A brochure of the route may be picked up at the Chamber of Commerce office on Alvarado Street between Del Monte Avenue and Franklin Street.

History here goes back to 1542, when the bay was first sighted by Juan Rodriquez Cabrillo. The Monterey mission was established by Junipero Serra in 1770 and the town was the capital of Alta California in 1775.

For a special bicycle ride, we will tour the entire coast line of the peninsula from Monterey to Carmel. Unfortunately, because bicycles are not allowed along 17-Mile Drive on weekends or holidays, this is a midweek trip. However, there is a cutoff for weekenders that slices the mileage but retains much of the spectacular scenery and allows a glimpse of Pacific Grove and marvelous vistas.

Our starting place will be Fisherman's Wharf in Monterey, easy to find via directional signs from Highway 1. There is a bike path and pedestrian way joining the wharf with the Monterey Bay Aquarium on Cannery Row. The path starts from the parking lot at the wharf. If you have escaped the pull of the shops, restaurants and boat rides of the wharf, you will find yourself having trouble escaping the pull of Cannery Row, where the old cannery plants of years gone by processed 200,000 tons

of sardines per year, and now house antique stores, boutiques, restaurants and art galleries. The Aquarium is a wonderful place, but if you stop there, you will not continue riding. Once past all these enticements, watch the sea for sea otters floating in the kelp, enjoying the same sights you are, and sea lions swimming by the rocks.

From Hopkins Marine Station northward you will be beside Pacific Grove Marine Gardens Park, where skin divers enjoy the underwater sights. The road is Ocean View Boulevard. There is a park all along the shore. Sea gulls and squirrels discuss in loud tones any scraps left from human lunches. The sea is a magnificent electric blue. As the road rounds from north toward the south, the Municipal Golf Course's green lawns are on the left and the blue and curling white of the sea on the right.

Ocean View becomes Sunset Drive. Beautiful homes take the place of the golf course greens. Sunset winds through Asilomar Conference Center

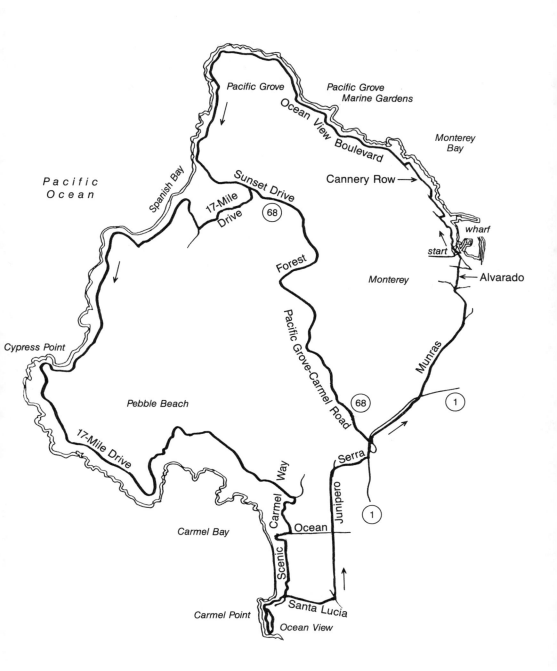

Pacific Grove

Pacific Grove
Marine Gardens

Ocean View Boulevard

Monterey
Bay

Pacific
Ocean

Spanish Bay

Sunset Drive

17-Mile
Drive

68

Cannery Row →

wharf

start

Forest

Monterey

Alvarado

Pacific Grove-Carmel Road

Cypress Point

Munras

68

1

Pebble Beach

Serra

17-Mile Drive

Carmel Way

Juniper

1

Carmel Bay

Ocean

Scenic

Carmel Point

Santa Lucia

Ocean View

25

CUTOFF

PACIFIC GROVE TO CARMEL

For sweeping views north and south, pedal up Sunset Drive, climbing out of Pacific Grove into Del Monte Forest. Sunset becomes Forest Avenue as you move up along the ridge that affords a sweeping view across the 17-Mile Drive coastline and Carmel Bay to Point Lobos. Then the view opens to the north across Monterey and Monterey Bay to Santa Cruz. The road becomes the Pacific Grove-Carmel Road. At Huckleberry Hill, you are at the high point and the road starts down toward Carmel. At the crossover at Highway 1, watch for the bike route on the east side of the highway and turn left. Pick up the commentary in the last paragraph (page 27).

away from the sea, but not for long. Asilomar was founded by the YWCA but is now owned by the state. The word means "refuge or retreat by the sea" and the grounds are used by many organizations for conferences.

At the intersection of Sunset Drive and 17-Mile Drive (6.1), whether it is a weekend or a weekday decides your route.

Turn right onto 17-Mile Drive toward Pebble Beach. 17-Mile Drive is a spectacular route, free for bicycles. Magnificent homes look across the Pacific to Hawaii and China. The road swings through a heavily wooded area and back to the sea at Spanish Bay. There are picnic tables here, and in the coves, the sea turns turquoise. Brilliant green Monterey Peninsula Country Club golf course comes down to meet combers as clear and transparent as colored glass.

Off Point Joe, ocean currents from north and south meet and churn in perpetual turbulence. Seal and Bird Rocks have restroom facilities, plus seals and cormorants, just as though they were hired for the spectators. One passes Spyglass Hill Golf Course and Cypress Point Golf Course. At Cypress Point Lookout, on a clear day, one can see Point Sur and the lighthouse, 20 miles south. The road pulls up and away from the shore, disappearing in a thick cypress grove of gnarled trees. Crocker Grove contains the largest and oldest Monterey cypress in the world. In the afternoon the sun glints off the sea, like a million diamonds caught in the branches of the trees.

At Pebble Beach there are shops and stores. There are hills in this area, giving a taste of Carmel ahead. Turn right at Carmel Way (15.1) and coast down to Ocean Avenue (15.7). Go right one block, loop around to the left and turn right on Scenic Road. White sand turns brilliant at Carmel Beach as you pedal along on the bluff above Carmel Bay. The houses here are small and jammed among the cypress and pines. Between Bay View and Stewart Way, on the left, is the sea side of Tor House and Hawk Tower, the poet Robinson Jeffers' home, and the first house on Carmel Point. He built the house and tower from the sea stones along the point.

The road then makes a hard left (17.1). Go up one block to Ocean View and turn left again, passing Jeffers' home on the left. There are tours here but they are reserved in advance through the Tor House Foundation. Turn left on Bay View back to Scenic and retrace along Scenic to Santa Lucia Avenue (17.7). Turn right and begin uphill work through Carmel. Turn left on Rio Road and Y right on Junipero Avenue (18.3). Junipero will give a good feeling of Carmel, the narrow winding streets that dodge around trees and follow the contour of the land. The downtown area is off to the left if you have any sightseeing left. There are several restaurants available for hungry bicyclists.

The road climbs upward to Serra Avenue (19.7). Turn right and go to the signal at Highway 1 (20.0). Turn left and you will be on a very busy highway. Bicyclists must exit at the Highway 68 off-ramp. Watch for the bike route that parallels the freeway on the east side. Safe from all harm, you will speed down the heights toward Monterey. The bike route continues, paralleling Munras Avenue through Dahvee Park. At the end of the park, Y left at the signal, staying on Munras to Alvarado Street. Traffic in the middle of town is heavy. Go straight across the Monterey Conference Center Plaza to the wharf (23.1).

10 THE HEART OF THE CENTRAL COAST INTERIOR

Distance: *83 miles*
Loop
Traffic: *light to moderate*
Rating: *difficult*

The studied money of Carmel Valley, the open reaches of the Santa Lucia Mountains and the sweep of the Salinas Valley are all encompassed in this long ride through the heart of central California. It is possible to break the ride in two, if you are willing to carry a change of clothes and a toothbrush. There are several resorts, lodges and inns in the Carmel Valley, plus very good restaurants to lure the weary bicyclist.

The trip starts near Soledad, where a car might be parked overnight in the care of a service station, should you take two days. The afternoon winds from the north up the Salinas Valley can be strong, so an early start is in order.

The route begins west of 101 at Arroyo Seco Road and Fort Romie (just south of Soledad). Head northwest on Fort Romie Road through the flatlands to Mission Nuestra Senora de la Soledad (Our Lady of Solitude) (1.5). It is the 13th in the chain of Franciscan missions.

Founded in 1791, it fell into disrepair and ruins. A rebuilding project began in 1955. The old adobe walls stand forlornly in front of the restoration. It is open from 10 to 4 each day except Tuesday.

Beyond the mission, jog to the left and right. Rich alluvial land is farmed on the left. This is called the Salad Bowl of the Nation. Salinas Valley crops include lettuce, celery, carrots, beans, potatoes, cauliflowers, and sugar beets. At the merging with River Road (3.8) keep northward, riding along the base of the Santa Lucia Mountains. To the west are the Gabilan Mountains and, just peeking out, the jagged rocks of Pinnacles National Monument. The road is pleasant, rolling, rural. Turn left following G17 at the intersection with Gonzales River Road (10.6). Following the foothills, River Road will go under the Highway 68 overpass. Turn left and pedal up the on-ramp toward Monterey (26.7). The road is heavily traveled, but there is a wide shoulder.

On the left is Toro Regional Park, where restroom facilities are available (28.3). The well-groomed park has pic-

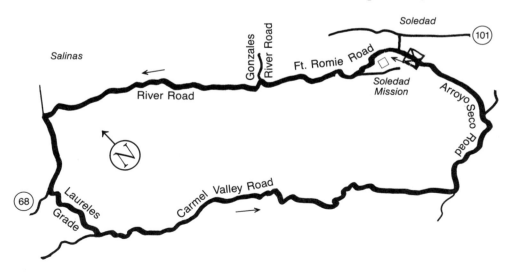

nic areas, some bicycle paths and hiking trails. Just beyond the park, on the right, is a small shopping center at Portola Road where supplies, refreshments or meals could be obtained.

The road begins a gentle climb up Canyon del Rey toward Monterey. At Laureles Grade (G20) (32.6) make a left turn onto a scenic highway. As the word "grade" indicates, there will be a good stiff pull of two and a half miles. At the top of the grade the road follows the ridge. The rolling ridges and peaks of the Santa Lucia Mountains stretch away in blues and purples to the south. The fun part starts with a two-and-a-half-mile drop into the Carmel Valley.

At Carmel Valley Road (G16) turn left (38.4). Here estate ranchettes and beautiful resorts line the road. The Carmel River runs beside the road, and the vegetation is lush. The road narrows as it moves away from the populated areas. The stream on the right is now Tularcitos Creek as the road climbs gradually into the mountains. Cottonwoods, sycamores, oaks line the roadside, The country opens up as the road climbs. This is a particularly lovely area in late winter and spring, when the hills are green and the wildflowers splash the land with color.

Spanish moss drapes from old oaks. The gradual climb becomes steeper at 50 miles, then flattens, and you will slip through cattle country, past large ranches. Up and down goes the road. The bubbling stream is Finch Creek. At 58 miles the road breaks on top. Looking south down through the Santa Lucias, the mountains roll away endlessly into the Ventana Wilderness. The peaks directly south are Bear Mountain and Junipero Serra, both over 5,000 feet in elevation.

Now it is downhill. There may be a cow or two in the road, so take care as you flee downward, past scraggly farms and small communities to Arroyo Seco Road (68.4). Turn left. Arroyo Seco means dry canyon, but during winter and spring the Arroyo Seco River is good-sized. This is indeed a drier country, caught in the rain shadow of the hills. Sagebrush and grasses are the prime native vegetation.

There is a short climb past tamer, more prosperous ranches, then down again to an intersection (75.0). Bear left on Arroyo Seco (G17). Ahead is the Salinas Valley; beyond, the Gabilan Mountains. The road swings north and sweeps over the alluvial fans spilling from the canyons. The farm land stretches to east and west, north and south, in the colors of growth or harvest. At the intersection of Arroyo Seco and Fort Romie Road, the trail comes to an end (83.1).

11 CARMEL TO BIG SUR

Distance: *51 miles*
Out and back
Traffic: *moderate to heavy*
Rating: *difficult*

Without a doubt the Big Sur Coast is one of the premier bicycling routes in the state. A good sample of the coast without making the commitment to go all the way to San Simeon is to bicycle from Carmel to Big Sur and return to Carmel. It is possible to take two days with a stay overnight at Big Sur, which will allow for leisurely bicycling, sightseeing along the rugged coast and exploring the Big Sur area. There are motels, inns, restaurants, and camping facilities there.

There is a problem or two with the route down the coast. One is the heavy weekend motor traffic, a second is the lack of shoulders at various locations along the way, and a third is a prevailing wind that will in all probability blow you to Big Sur but hinder your return. All the problems, however, can be surmounted for a chance to bicycle this splendid coastline.

The route begins south of Carmel at the intersection of Highway 1 and Rio Road. Pedal past the artichoke patch, up the hill and down to Carmel River State Beach for the first glimpse of the sea, with Point Lobos jutting westward.

Point Lobos is a state reserve of intense natural beauty, where rock and shore, coves and tidepools, and a rugged stand of Monterey cypress await the wary pedaler. It would be easy to get off the bicycle right here (1.9).

Continuing up through Carmel Highlands with art galleries on the left and sculptured cypress on the right, the road twists and turns past a number of resort lodges. There is no shoulder, but the traffic moves slowly.

The road swings out toward the sea. At Malpaso Creek the mileage is 4.4. The grand jumble of steep-sided mountains, dark in its vegetation and rock,

cuts down to the sea and then is met by the deep blue of the Pacific breaking in white foam atop translucent green combers. The rocks and headlands are stark against the sea. Below the road, off your right ankle, keyhold rocks stand steady in the frothing surge.

Bixby Creek Bridge (12.5) is one of the most easily recognized of the 29 bridges along the coast. It is the longest concrete arch span in the world, 718 feet long, 260 feet above the creek.

Each headland must be climbed over, the road climbing up and then swinging down to cross another canyon. If you are lucky the day is brilliantly clear, but

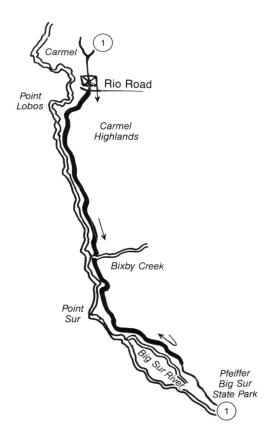

it may be that the fog is hanging over the road, or making up on the sea, turning the sun into a ghost moon. The fog may be high, shrouding the hilltops, or it may hang over the road, making it a tunnel through which to ride, the sound of the sea the only way to know that off there, to the right, are the Hawaiian Islands and, beyond that, China.

There is a long climb after Bixby with a view from which the lighthouse at Point Sur can be seen. The road drops down to the Little Sur River (15.9) and then climbs up and flattens by the Point Sur Light Station. Established in 1889, the automatic light warns passing ships for a distance of 25 miles. A causeway connects the U.S. Naval station, on a huge hump of headland, with the shore (18.4).

The road moves inland, up a canyon filled with redwoods, and beside the Big Sur River. Andrew Molera State Park is located at the river mouth. Big Sur Village and Fernwood have campgrounds, restaurants, motels; Pfeiffer Big Sur State Park (25.0) has campgrounds and a lodge.

The area was first settled about 1860, then there were some small farms, and finally the state acquired the property for a park in 1934. State Highway 1 was completed in 1937 after 18 years of work, allowing access to the area. Before the highway, it took 11 hours to get to Big Sur from Monterey over a wagon road. Indeed, the first settlers had to pack in over a rough trail, a four-day trip.

The return trip out of the redwoods and cedars sends you back to civilization and Carmel, the wide sweep of Carmel Bay and the Monterey Peninsula. On the right is the Carmelite Monastery. Pedal up the last knoll and down to Rio Road (50.7) to complete a glimpse of what lies farther south.

12 WEST PINNACLES HILL CLIMB

Distance: *24 miles*
Out and back
Traffic: *light*
Rating: *difficult*

Pinnacles National Monument is a hikers' paradise in fall, winter and spring — particularly spring, when the hills are covered with green grass and splashed with wildflowers. The road into West Pinnacles is a bicyclists' challenge, climbing some 1,500 feet in 12 miles. It is also very hot and dry during the summer. At road's end, Chaparral, there are excellent views of the last remnants of this ancient volcano, great buttresses against the sky.

The route starts in Soledad, just off Highway 101. Soledad, population 6,700, is the oldest settlement in the Salinas Valley. It was established at the founding of the Soledad Mission in 1791.

Start at East and Front streets, where Highway 146 leads east out of town. Turn right at Metz Road (0.3), following Highway 146 toward Pinnacles. Quickly the road is out of town and past the large Paul Masson Pinnacles Vineyard complex. There are miles of vineyards in the area, and in the fall the musky smell of grapes and wines cuts the air.

Turn left at the West Pinnacles sign (2.9). This is not the most popular entrance to Pinnacles, and the road is not heavily traveled. As the road begins to climb, the Salinas Valley opens up with views north and south and across the way to the Santa Lucia Mountains. Often the air is clear and brilliant, for the winds sweep down the Salinas Valley, and metropolitan areas are far away. If the weather is good, the sky will be a soft baby blue. The smells are of sage and grasses.

The uphill is gentle for five miles, gradually steepening. The scrub oak is laden with mistletoe, indicating the trees are weakening in this area of sparse rainfall. Soon the pinnacles will be sighted; then the country will open and the view will extend to the north along the Gabilan Mountains and west to the Santa Lucias. The road begins to drop into the national monument, and Highway 146 ends. The road narrows and drops into Chaparral, where there are picnic and restroom facilities (12.1), and the trails begin into the peaks. Camping is allowed Monday through Thursday.

There is one short trail, a mile in length, into the Balconies Cliffs and Caves. Take a flashlight if you plan to

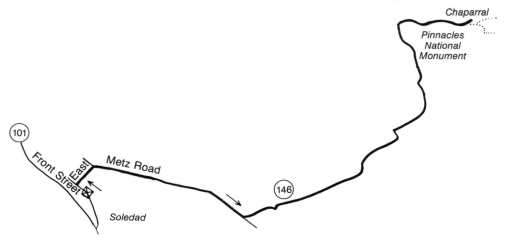

hike in the caves.

The San Andreas Fault runs through the middle of Pinnacles National Monument. Some 23½ million years ago the volcano boiled tons of rock and lava through fissures and covered the countryside. Then the tectonic plates began pushing under and over each other and moving north and south. Riding on the rim, the old volcano remnant moved 195 miles northwest of its original site and has been eroded to shape the jagged rock formations.

The road back works its way up from Chaparral about two miles and then down to Soledad.

Follow Highway 146 back to Soledad (24.1).

13 BITTERWATER TO EAST PINNACLES

Distance: *41 miles*
Out and back
Traffic: *light to moderate*
Rating: *easy to moderate*

The extraordinary formations of an ancient volcano are the destination of this ride out of King City through the rolling landscape of the Gabilan Mountains. It is possible to start in King City and ride to Bitterwater, which will add 30 miles to the total distance of the trip, or to start in Bitterwater for an easier day of it. Be advised: there is but one store along the way and it is not open at all hours, or even every day.

To get to Bitterwater, take G13 at King City from Highway 101, the Bitterwater Road, heading northeast. It is 15 miles up a pleasant two-lane road with a wide shoulder for bicycling.

The Gabilans are the sunny hills of Steinbeck's *East of Eden.* If the weather is good, the sky will be a crystal blue, for the winds wipe it clean and the brown air of the cities is far distant. In the spring the sweep of the hills and mountains ranges from lightest yellow-green to deepest blue-green.

In Bitterwater, which is little more than an intersection with Highway 25, head north (to the left) through an upland valley cupped in the sage-covered hills. The road turns to cross the valley. At the intersection with the Clear Creek Road, the old wagon road to Coalinga, turn left (2.0), staying on Highway 25 toward East Pinnacles. There is little or no shoulder and on weekends during the spring the traffic can be moderate along this twisting road. The summer can be hot, very hot, in the 90s and 100s, but the fall is fine riding. The weather grows iffy but is often delightful in winter. The spring is the time of year that the country shows off, with hills a myriad of green and wildflowers belying a drab world. It is dry-land farming through the Little Rabbit and Dry Lake valleys as the road winds in and out and

up and down. The fields turn green velvet in the spring and buttered-toast velvet in the summer.

The intersection with the road to San Benito is 10.8. The area is worth exploring if you have the time and inclination. Be warned: San Benito is a group of houses, the old Jefferson School, a new school, and a corral. The road branches at San Benito left and right. The right road turns to dirt in some eight miles but moves along the bluffs above the San Benito River through a beautiful valley.

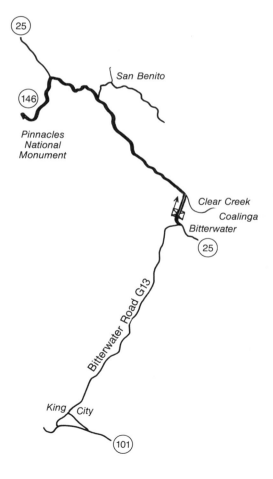

34

After a climb over a saddle beyond the San Benito cutoff you can catch a glimpse of the buttresses of the Pinnacles ahead. At the intersection with Highway 146, turn left (13.8), following the Pinnacles sign. The San Andreas fault lies down the middle of Bear Valley, near a group of white farm buildings. The only camping allowed in the area is at the Pinnacles Campground ($5 per site) on the left (16.8) where a store is located. The Valley pinches into a narrow canyon, then around a corner, and suddenly the Pinnacles loom along the skyline. At the turn to the Visitor's Center, go left (18.4) and climb along the side of a steep hill to the parking lot (20.6).

Here the shade of the pines and oaks and a tiny stream cool visitors. The hiking trails head up into the hills. In fact, hiking is the only way to see this core of an ancient volcano. One of the best trails is the Moses Spring Trail, which is 0.7 mile up (and 0.7 mile back), and will give you a chance to go through the Bear Gulch Caves. Take a flashlight if possible.

Be sure and look in the Visitor's Center exhibit and discover that the other part of this old volcano is now near Lancaster on the east side of the San Andreas fault. The slippage is some 195 miles. The "southern" rock formations are buried under rounded hills, but here the "northern" rocks are exposed, poking craggy fingers in the blue of the sky.

The ranger claimed the wildflowers bring people like they bring bees, so the area is liable to be swarming with flower buffs each weekend between February and June. The area was set aside as a national monument in 1908 by Teddy Roosevelt.

After exploring, it is back on the bikes, northeast on Highway 146 with a right turn at Highway 25 (27.4). Another right turn at Clear Creek Road (39.2) and two more miles to Bitterwater (41.2) will return you to your car. If you are bicycling from King City, the total mileage is 71.

14 SAN ANTONIO MISSION

Distance: *45 miles*
Semi-loop
Traffic: *light to moderate*
Rating: *moderate*

Tucked away off main highways is the third of California's Franciscan missions, San Antonio de Padua. Founded in 1771 and in a fine state of restoration, the mission resides now in the middle of Hunter Liggett Military Reservation.

The missions tell a story of early success, secularization, decline, often total neglect, ruin, then restoration. So it is with San Antonio. The mission settles quietly in the Valley of the Oaks, with many outbuildings marked, including the old gristmill, the Indian laundry, the wells, the water wheel, wine vat and aqueduct system. A sense of what early California was like pervades. There is a picnic area, and one should allow at least an hour to explore the grounds and mission.

The journey to the past will begin west of King City at the intersection of Highway 101 and Jolon Road (G14). Head south on Jolon, up a little hill past the historical landmark for the mission. There is a small store where picnic supplies might be picked up for the journey. The road slips across the alluvial fans that spill out of the Santa Lucia Mountain canyons and grow fine crops. The road leads into the rolling hills with cattle grazing and oil pumping. Spring time brings brilliant greens and bright wildflowers; late spring and summer bring beige velvet set against the dark green of the scrubs and oaks. A pull into the hills and a two-mile downhill brings one into Hunter Liggett, where the valley broadens and an oak forest weeps Spanish moss. Jolon is believed to be an Indian word for "Valley of the Dead Oaks."

Just outside Jolon, where the sign says the population is 66, are the ruins of the two-story Dutton Hotel (17.0). The adobe is protected by a shelter, but lit-

tle remains of what used to be the hub of a busy stage stop on El Camino Real. The hotel was built in 1849 and went out of business in 1929.

Turn right on Mission Drive at 17.4. There is a small shopping center if supplies are running short. The entrance to Hunter Liggett is just beyond. The military reservation was purchased from William Randolph Hearst in 1940.

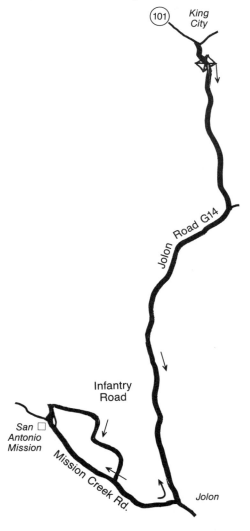

It comprises 170,000 acres and is named after General Hunter Liggett, World War I troop commander and General Pershing's chief of staff.

After passing the military guard, the road leads along the Valley of the Oaks through military facilities and equipment. Warning: once I was not allowed to bicycle on the reservation because of military maneuvers. The reservation is home for the Combat Development Experimentation Command field laboratory. On the right, high on the bluff, is Hearst's former hunting lodge, Hacienda, now the headquarters for the Army. The lovely Spanish-style building catches the sunlight and gleams pure white against the hills behind.

The mission is on the left (23.0), under quiet oaks, a contrast to the military focus all about. It is open Monday through Saturday, 9:30 a.m. to 4:30 p.m., and on Sundays from 11 a.m. to 5 p.m. The grounds are extensive and well-marked. The mission was considered the most prosperous and populated of the chain of 21 founded by Franciscan fathers between 1769 and 1823.

The return to Highway 101 starts on Mission Creek Road and turns left on Infantry Road. Pedal up to the Hacienda, then continue straight ahead on Infantry Road, past the PX and up a short hill to roll through the countryside and back to Mission Road (25.1). Turn left and return to Jolon (28.1). Left again on Jolon Road and return to the start at Highway 101.

The total mileage for the trip is 45.3.

15 PARIS LAKE

Distance: *24 miles*
Loop
Traffic: *light*
Rating: *easy to moderate*

Sometimes . . . well, actually, many times, some hidden valley, unknown to the busy world of streaming automobiles and tall skyscrapers, makes for good bicycling. So it is with Paris Valley, located between two half-forgotten towns, San Lucas and San Ardo, in the hills just east of the Salinas River.

The ride starts in San Ardo, which has a motel and a restaurant, and can be reached east of Highway 101. The point of departure is Our Lady of Ransom

Catholic Church on Cattlemen Road.

San Ardo is a corruption of the name San Bernardo and is named after the huge ranch that still dominates the area. The population of the town is 500, and it is a sheep and cattle raising center. There are rich oil fields to the south and northeast, discovered in 1947, that are bringing additional life to the community. The plat was filed in 1887, and the town dates from that period.

Leaving San Ardo, head west on Cattlemen Road, which becomes the Paris Valley Road as it goes under the freeway. Turn right at Paris Valley and Dudley Road, heading up into the low-lying foothills of the Santa Lucia Mountains. The open, sunny hills part for the narrow country road. Old farm houses and barns lean against one another.

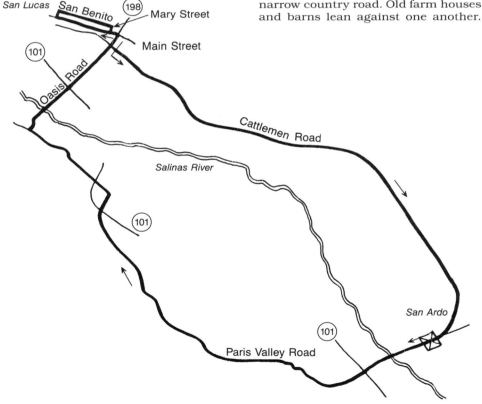

Again, spring can be spectacular with lupines and poppies splashing hillsides and road margins, and oats and barley stretching varied greens against the blue of the sky. Hawks laze through the air and red-winged blackbirds watch from wire fences. The road slips out of the upland valley and begins a descent. Ahead is the Salinas Valley and river and the white ribbon of 101.

Paris Valley Road crosses the freeway (7.7) and runs below a bluff. It moves up and down in undulating curves and then turns right onto Oasis Road (10.8), which winds down to the Salinas River to cross on the narrow steel girder bridge. For a rest and a chance to dip your toes in the Salinas River (if it is running water instead of sand), there is access to the river from near the bridge. Slip under the 101 Freeway (11.8) and Oasis becomes Highway 198. For a tour into San Lucas, turn left onto Main Street (12.4).

San Lucas boasts a population nearing 200 and was once a Basque sheepherder stronghold. The town is a group of small residences and has an old general store of interest, plus a school and a church. Just before Main Street dead-ends at an old barn, turn right on San Lucas (13.0) and then right again on San Benito. At Mary Street, turn right (13.5), and then left onto Main and right onto Highway 198 and left onto Cattlemen Road (13.8). Out of town, on the left, is the community cemetery, dominated by a monument to Albert Trescony, founder of San Lucas and a benefactor of the Basques.

Cattlemen Road is the old highway which runs along below the bluff where the railroad track thunders before an on-coming train. The afternoon wind should be straight at your back. The road is almost straight, almost flat and cuts through farming areas to San Ardo and the start (23.9).

16 LITTLE TOWNS—JOLON, SAN LUCAS, LOCKWOOD

Distance: *41 miles*
Loop
Traffic: *light to moderate*
Rating: *moderate*

Three tiny towns, forgotten by progress and passed over by freeways, are connected by the rolling land of the Santa Lucia Mountain foothills. Jolon, population 66, once a busy stage stop; Lockwood, population 123, once a homestead center; and San Lucas, population 200, once a thriving farming center, sleep in the midday sun, pleased perhaps to have escaped the frenetic pace of modern American life. Sleeping as they do, they are perfect hubs for a bicycle trip that is spectacular in spring, merely glorious in fall and winter, and perhaps a little hot in midsummer.

With easy access from Highway 101 to San Lucas, our route will begin in this tiny town, settled in the late 1800s by Alfred Trescony. Trescony was a benefactor of Basque sheepherders bringing bands of sheep to the Salinas Valley from the San Joaquin. There is a small restaurant but no motels. King City to the north and San Ardo to the

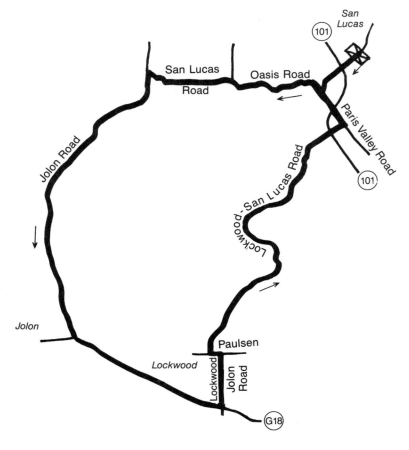

south have motels, however, and several rides are available in the area, starting at both King City and San Ardo.

Leaving the corner of Main Street and Highway 198 in San Lucas, pedal south toward Highway 101. Slip under the freeway and across the Salinas River. The highway becomes Oasis Road and climbs up from the river flood plain onto the bluffs, where it intersects with the Lockwood-Jolon Road/Paris Valley Road (1.6) and turns right and then swings left. New vineyards seem to sprout from every hillock. Wine may take over as the new liquid gold of the area.

The winding old country road has little or no traffic and moves leisurely up a shallow valley and over a little ridge, back into the Santa Lucias. At the juncture with San Lucas Road (4.9), continue straight ahead on San Lucas on a steady, gradual uphill. The road surface is rough and slowly becomes steeper as it nears the top. There is a break in the ridge, the top is gained, and then a steep and straight downhill ride to the Jolon Road, G14 (7.2), is followed by a left turn. There is moderate traffic headed toward Hunter Liggett Military Reservation along this road. The Jolon Grade will test your gearing, or your legs.

The route moves into the hills, where a wide valley harbors groves of oak struggling under Spanish moss. Cattle and sheep graze on the grasses in spring and summer, and struggle with tidbit blades in fall and winter. Just before entering Jolon, an adobe ruin sits at the right side of the road, all that remains of the Dutton Hotel, built in 1849 and once the hub of a busy stagecoach stop on El Camino Real. It was in use until 1929, but in the ensuing 60 years, rain and wind and biting frost have taken their tolls, and little but a heap of mud remains. It is, however, a national landmark, and may have been the model for the stone castle in John Steinbeck's short story "The Murder." Jolon itself is the background for Steinbeck's *To a God Unknown.*

At Jolon, where there is a small shopping center, Y left (18.7), continuing on G14 to Lockwood. The road is straight and determined along this upland valley rimmed by low hills. At the Lockwood store and cafe, on the corner of the Lockwood-Jolon Road, turn left, north (24.2). Lockwood was originally homesteaded in 1874 and was reported to be a lively center where grain and wheat were (and are) grown. The post office, general store and cafe are about all that is left of the original town.

The road slips through the houses of Lockwood and up a gradual grade past the school. Turn left at Paulsen and then right onto the Lockwood-San Lucas Road (26.7) to pedal out of town and away from civilization into the Santa Lucias' rolling and rounded hills. Sheep graze in spring, like dirty cotton balls sprinkled on the green grass.

Slowly the hills steepen as the narrow, two-lane country road moves through acres of barley and oats. The gradient tops out after six miles with a long downhill. Ahead is the dark Gabilan Range to the northeast. Cattle graze the hills, turning fat and sleek before your eyes. The quiet is broken by a whisper of a breeze, the whir of the bicycle, the call of a hawk. As the valley opens out, Highway 101 can be seen far ahead and the white silo of San Lucas gleams in the afternoon sun.

Duck under Highway 101 (38.1) and turn left on the Lockwood-San Lucas/Paris Valley Road along the bluffs above the Salinas River. The two-lane road turns right onto Oasis (39.4). The road winds down to the Salinas River and crosses on a narrow steel bridge with access to the water. Under the freeway (40.4) and the road becomes Highway 198 and returns to San Lucas by going under the old highway to Main Street (41).

17 SAN ANTONIO LAKE

Distance: *53 miles*
Loop
Traffic: *light to moderate*
Rating: *difficult*

The loop around San Antonio Lake is a natural, with tantalizing views of both San Antonio and Nacimiento lakes, a visit to San Antonio, and a ride through the sprawling hills of Central California. The twin lakes crawl up canyons in the Santa Lucia Mountains behind dams on the San Antonio and the Nacimiento rivers. The road is the "high road," well above the lakes for the most part, but a stellar view of Nacimiento occurs at one spot, the road dips down to San Antonio at another, and a short and easy side trip will take the bicyclist down to a picnic area, campground and marina at the latter. So there is the possibility of camping along the way for a weekend trip.

The loop begins at Highway 101 north of Bradley and Camp Roberts. Take the Nacimiento and San Antonio Lakes-Jolon exit west off Highway 101 and turn immediately south on G19 toward Nacimiento Lake and the south shore of San Antonio. This is a particularly beautiful ride during spring when the grasses are green, the oaks are in new leaf and the wildflowers are splashing painter's easel colors across the landscape. It is also a delight in fall and, if the winter weather is not dripping, in winter. Summer gets a little hot for much more than lounging by the lake and dabbling feet and body in the water.

Nacimiento Lake Road winds up through rolling hills past fields of oats and barley. Doves dart through the air with rushes of wind over wing feathers. The road slopes down off the uplands. The mountains rimming the uplands are dark blue — purple mountains majesty. The road crosses the San Antonio River (5.0) on a steel girder bridge that

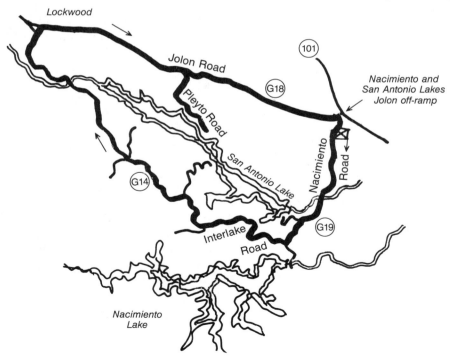

Lockwood

Jolon Road

101

Pleyto Road

Nacimiento and
San Antonio Lakes
Jolon off-ramp

G18

San Antonio Lake

Nacimiento Road

G14

Interlake
Road

G19

Nacimiento
Lake

chatters hands numb and then begins a pull up toward the dam. Turn left, remaining on G19 (6.8) just before reaching the dam and take a rough surface road up, ever up, to top out (8.5) and make a right turn onto G14, Interlake Road. The road continues up with a view of San Antonio to the right in the distance, and on the left, close by, sprawling Nacimiento Lake, cupped in dusky blue hills. The road continues still upward for a total of three and a half miles and then there is a swooping downhill on that rough road.

At the bottom of the downhill an arm of San Antonio clutches at the lake road, which turns upward again. At Bee Rock there is a store where supplies can be purchased. The road to the south shore angles to the right (16.1), where there are a marina, store and campgrounds. However, for this ride we will continue to the north shore for a rendezvous with the water.

The fields are full of fat squirrels and a whisper-quiet bicycle will rouse a number of them with a start. The road climbs short ridges and drops into shallow valleys and then begins a long, gentle downhill to cross the upper reaches of the San Antonio River and pull into Lockwood (28.5) at the Jolon Road. There is a cafe and store.

At the community of Lockwood, turn right on G18, Jolon Road. The wide two-lane road slips through the broad valley rimmed by low, rolling hills covered with sage. The area is farmed for oats and barley, brilliant green in spring, shading to velvet browns in summer and then cut and baled.

Occasional glimpses of the lake can be caught off in the distance. At Pleyto Road (34.5), turn right to go down to the lake. The road is an easy downhill for about five miles, with an easy return. There is a day use fee for bicyclists and camping is additional. Up and over a sudden ridge, there is a small store at the marina, and many areas for picnicking. The lake itself is a long, narrow body of blue water covering almost 6,000 acres and is part of the Monterey County Flood Control and Water Conservation District. Oak-dotted peninsulas jut into the lake.

Return to Jolon Road (44.4) and turn right to continue through the rolling terrain, with good strong uphills followed by swift downhill rides, opening out into the Hames Valley. The elevation drops through ranch areas to 101 (53.1).

18 NACIMIENTO LAKE AND SAN MIGUEL

Distance: *39 miles*
Loop
Traffic: *light to moderate*
Rating: *difficult*

Not much more than a touch of Naci-miento Lake will be the reward for a ride through the Santa Lucia Mountains on this loop around Camp Roberts Military Reservation, starting in the mission town of San Miguel. Still, any excuse for a good strong ride through the Central Coast hills is worthwhile. There is camping overnight at the lake, however, should a break be wished.

This starting point will be at Mission San Miguel Arcangel, just off Highway 101 in the town of San Miguel. There are restaurants and a motel as the town begins restoration in the hope of luring tourists off the highway. The town itself was once located south of the mission, but after a fire in 1887 that destroyed the business district, it was moved to its present site. It had two booms, one when the railroad came and another during World War II when Camp Roberts was operating at full capacity. Population was then 4,000 — now it numbers about 900.

The mission is well worth a lengthy visit. Founded in 1797, the 16th of the chain of 21 California missions, Mission San Miguel is famed for its cactus garden and lovely courtyard. It fell into disrepair after secularization in 1836, but has been restored by the Fran-ciscans beginning in 1929. Its interior is said to be the best preserved of any in the state, with original paintings done by the Indians. The museum at the mission is open from 10 a.m. to 5 p.m. daily.

Also of interest in San Miguel is the Rios-Caledonia Adobe, just south of the mission. Built in 1846, it later became the Caledonia Inn and had as its guests, among others, the Dalton Brothers, the James Brothers, and Joaquin Murieta. It has been restored and is open 10 a.m. to 4 p.m. Wednesday through Sunday.

A warning about bicycling this route: It can only be run counter-clockwise because there is no access to San Marcos Road from the freeway. You can, however, get on the freeway from San Marcos.

Starting from the mission, head north on Mission Drive toward 101 Freeway North. The route takes one along the main street. The road moves slowly out of town and up toward the freeway, which descends to meet it (2.7). Once on the freeway, it is moderate traffic moving rapidly on a four-lane divided highway with a wide shoulder. Freeway travel is always marginally exciting because of fast-moving trucks and automobiles. More to be endured than enjoyed, the freeway's attributes are that it is fast, level, and relatively safe with high visibility and wide shoulders. It does not, thank heaven, last forever.

Camp Roberts, looking semiabandon-ed most of the time, is on the left. It is a 44,000-acre training camp, now used by the National Guard but was, during World War II, the largest center of its kind in the world. Its slogan is, "We are the most active inactive post in the Army."

The freeway passes over the Naci-miento River (6.5). Just beyond is a rest area with restroom facilities (7.2). Take the San Antonio Lake, G14, G18, Fort Hunter Liggett, Jolon exit (12.6). Slip under the freeway and turn left onto G19, Nacimiento Lake Road (13.2). The change is abrupt from freeway to a lit-tle country road, barely two-lane, with no shoulder and no markings and no traffic. The road dances through a small canyon and then climbs easily up into a wide upland valley with rolling fields of grain, sparkling green in the late winter and spring, velvet brown in ear-ly summer, and square for the rest of the year. The road comes off the uplands, down into the valley where the San An-tonio River is crossed (18.2) over a steel

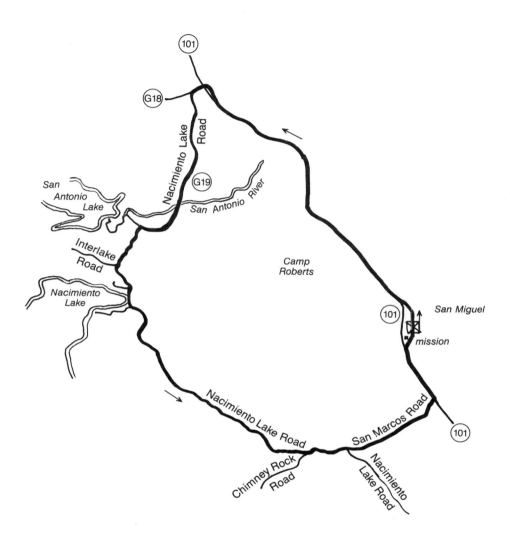

girder bridge.

The road moves up the valley. Turn left, staying on Nacimiento Lake Road (20.0) as the road begins a climb to the top of the canyon walls holding San Antonio Dam. The road not taken climbs to a vista point overlooking San Antonio Lake and is about a mile and a half to the top.

Nacimiento Lake Road struggles up the canyon on a rough surface for a mile and a half. Go straight ahead at the in- tersection with Interlake Road, continu- ing on Nacimiento Lake Road (21.7). A bobcat may lope across the road and in the spring the area is wild blue in lupine. Drop down to Nacimiento Dam and pedal across (23.0). Nacimiento Lake Resort is to the right just over the dam. There is an $8 fee for camping overnight, and the road into the camp- grounds is about a mile. The lake itself is caught in a steep canyon and boasts 165 miles of shoreline. Nacimiento

45

means "source." The name was given to the river by the Portola Expedition in 1769.

Continuing on past the dam (which is the first and last look at the lake, so if you want to linger for a break, or for lunch, do so here), the road climbs up the scenic highway with minimal shoulders. A short steep ascent results in a steep downhill, which is nice, because another uphill awaits as the road works its way through the Santa Lucia Range of the Coast Range (and don't ask me how that works).

At the intersection with Chimney Rock Road, turn left, remaining on Nacimiento Lake Road toward Paso Robles (30.4). A long straight downhill with a shoulder will cease (for the bicyclist) with a left turn onto San Marcos Road (32.3).

The road is up and down and back and forth through vineyards and grasslands. Sycamores crowd down near a stream, and killdeer flash their whites and grays. The road slips through the hills toward the Salinas River and comes to the 101 Freeway (37.3). Turn left toward San Miguel and exit on the San Miguel off-ramp (38.5) to the mission and the end of the trip (38.9).

19 SAN SIMEON AND HEARST CASTLE

Distance: *58 miles*
Out and back
Traffic: *light to moderate*
Rating: *moderate*
Side trip: *26 miles, easy to difficult*

Hearst Castle is the most popular of California State Parks, perched as it is high on a hill above San Simeon and filled with furnishings and art work from the castles of Europe. The gardens are exquisite, the lovely pools incomparable, the buildings and interiors seemingly improbable.

And Morro Bay to San Simeon is a nice bicycle ride.

This trip can be approached in several ways. One is as a delicious manner of getting to Hearst Castle to take a tour of the buildings and grounds. The second is as a bicycle ride along the coast and through the foothills of the Central Coast area. And a third would be to break the long ride plus side trip by camping or moteling. If the first is on the agenda, be forewarned that reservations are necessary for specific tours. If you do it in one day, pick a day and an hour that will give you time to pedal there, tour and pedal back. Tickets for tours are available through Ticketron. Although there is a chance to pick up tour tickets at the castle, it is a small chance indeed, particularly on weekends and during the summer.

The bicycle ride by itself is worth the effort, however, and the tiny town of San Simeon does boast a State Historical Landmark. A side trip will take the bicyclist further up the coast to Ragged Point, where the flat or slightly rolling shoreline will give way to the rugged and difficult ride along the Big Sur Coast. It is a pleasant coast indeed, and an early start is always recommended to avoid if possible any stray strands of wind that sweep out of the northwest.

Morro Bay has a number of motels and restaurants and is the town sheltered at the base of "The Gibraltar of the Pacific," Morro Rock. The huge, hulking rock, once a volcanic plug, rears out of the sea almost 600 feet. The town itself was founded in 1870 and has become a center for seafood, fishing, wildlife watching, and boating.

Starting at the intersection of Highway 1 and Main Street, where Main ducks under the freeway, head north on Main. The street parallels the freeway through a business district. Traffic is not heavy and the going flat. At Yerba Buena Avenue (2.3), jog left onto the highway, which has wide shoulders. The road follows the contours of Estero Bay to Cayucos. Take the Cayucos exit to go through town (5.1), thus avoiding the hill. Cayucos used to be a shipping port, with a wharf that was famous for shipping cheeses and dairy products from nearby farms. The town was founded in 1867, and the wharf built in 1875. Pedal along the main street and out of town on the north to slip back onto the freeway (6.9).

North of Cayucos the highway moves inland around Point Estero and past the town of Harmony (population 18), once a dairy center famous for its cheese (14.2). Now some of the old buildings have been restored and it features art galleries, antique stores and a restaurant.

The hills begin to roll and there is a climb into the outskirts of Cambria. At the Cambria Village sign, turn right onto Main Street to zip downhill and ride through the town of Cambria. Another popular resort town, Cambria was founded about 1869 as a fishing and mining center. It now harbors artists by the score and many buildings along the main street are restorations housing art galleries, restaurants, antique stores and other points of interest. Exit off Main and back onto Highway 1 (20.7) and continue toward San Simeon. From here the road hugs the shore and the way is flat.

Far up on a peak of the Santa Lucia

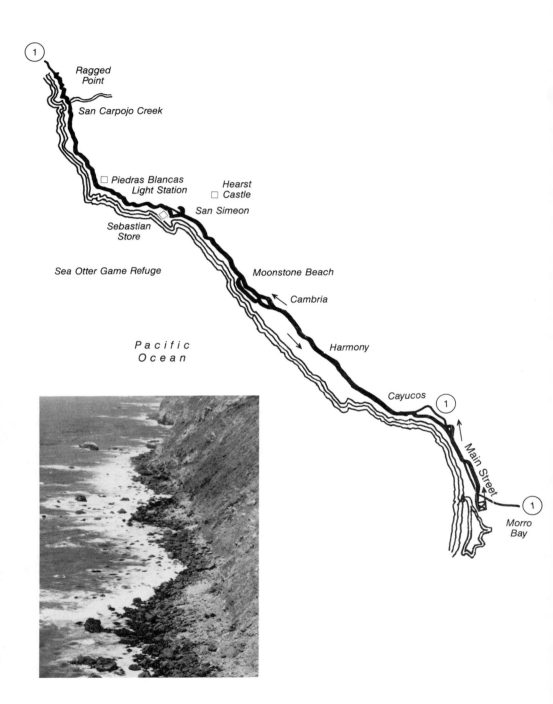

1

Ragged
Point

San Carpojo Creek

□ Piedras Blancas
Light Station

Hearst
□ Castle

San Simeon

Sebastian
Store

Sea Otter Game Refuge

Moonstone Beach

Cambria

Pacific
Ocean

Harmony

Cayucos

1

Main Street

1

Morro
Bay

RAGGED POINT

The road to Ragged Point is rated difficult because of one climb at the very end of the ride, but the rest of the way is easy to moderate and will follow along the seashore for miles. One point of interest is Piedras Blancas, where the light station is located, which is only about five and a half miles.

There is an easy hill out of San Simeon, across a low headland, which slips back to the sea. Waves dash against the low bluffs. Piedras Blancas Lighthouse was built in 1874 and, fully automated, is operated by the Coast Guard. It is not open to the public. It is built on the point originally named Piedra Blanca (white stone) by Cabrillo in 1542.

About a mile beyond is the settlement of Piedras Blancas, which has a small cafe and motel. All along this coast is a sea otter game refuge, part of a very successful effort to bring the sea otter back from near extinction.

At San Carpojo Creek the easy riding ends, and there is a rugged mile and a half pull up to Ragged Point, where there are an inn and a snack shack. The road is typical of what lies ahead along the Big Sur Coast, one of the most magnificent in the world, and one of the most difficult to bicycle. The road has virtually no shoulder and is one climb followed by another. From Ragged Point there is a view up that coast, and a steep trail down to the roaring surf below. Returning to San Simeon, the mileage is 25.6.

Mountains is the white wonder of Hearst Castle. The right turn (27.7) into the parking lot (28.2) will find you in a beehive of activity as a few of the one and a half million visitors per year await their turns on the buses that take them to the Enchanted Hill, La Cuesta Encantada. The house itself is La Casa Grande, built by publisher William Randolph Hearst. The house was begun in 1922 and never finished. It has over 100 rooms, four guest "cottages," each fit for a king, and pieces of art too numerous to catalog here. It is worth every minute you can spend, a most intriguing, egomaniacal edifice. Thank heaven for egomaniacs: for the rest of us they make the world a little more exciting.

There is a snack bar here. However, it might be more worthwhile to ride back down to Highway 1 (28.9) and cross it to go into San Simeon. There is camping at Hearst Memorial State Beach. Following the road into San Simeon, stop at Sebastian's, built in 1873, where lunches can be obtained. The little town was once a whaling center for ships sheltering in San Simeon Bay. Continue on up the road where it intersects with Highway 1 (29.5).

Heading south from San Simeon's north exit on Highway 1, turn right onto Moonstone Beach (35.4). This is part of San Simeon Beach State Park, where there are camping, picnic and restroom facilities. Moonstone Beach is named for the moonstones found along its shore.

There are motels close to Cambria, and restaurants. At Highway 1, turn right (37.6) and pedal up the hill past Cambria and along the uplands to Cayucos. Exit right onto North Ocean (51.4) and continue through town, again exiting onto Highway 1 (53.2). Continue south to Morro Bay and the Main Street off-ramp (first Morro Bay exit) at 58.3.

20 FOLLOWING TWO RIVER ROADS

Distance: *37 miles*
Loop
Traffic: *light to moderate*
Rating: *moderate*

Although the thought of river roads brings to mind the swish and gurgle of water behind a line of trees, for six months out of the year neither of these rivers has water in it. The trees are there, however, and usually shade. But the Salinas and Estrella rivers are not the usual Mississippis. They are very much rivers of semiarid Central California. All of this does not make the ride any less delightful, particularly with a trip to San Miguel added. And if you are lucky, the water will be running and you can steal some time along the banks, dabbling tired feet. This area can be hot in summer, just when you need to dabble feet, and rarely does the river run then.

The starting point will be in Paso Robles, a city of about 16,400 that serves as a hub for traffic moving along Highways 101 and 46. Paso Robles is the leading city of north San Luis Obispo County. It is an agricultural center, with wheat and almonds among its most popular crops. It grew up around a hot springs that became a popular tourist spa. The hot springs were in use from the early 1800s, and became a resort about 1860. Paso Robles was a village by 1883 and was incorporated as a city in 1889. It has many hotels and restaurants and is a good base for bicycling operations.

Pedal east on Highway 46 from 101 Freeway. Turn right onto Union Road (2.0) for a pedal through the countryside, although one could proceed for a smoother ride on Highway 46 to Estrella. It will be a mile and a half shorter. Union crosses Dry Creek on a steel girder bridge and roller coasters across the grassy landscape that resembles a green chenille bedspread in spring.

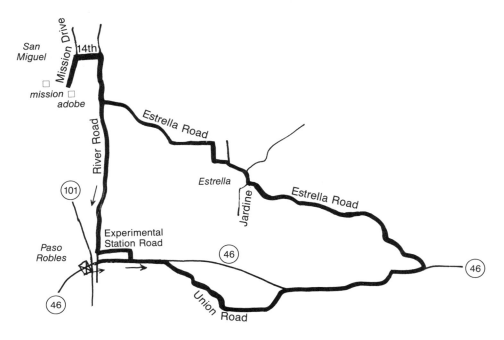

At Highway 46, turn right (9.6). A mile beyond, after a short downhill just before crossing the Estrella River bridge, turn left on Estrella Road (10.8). The road parallels the Estrella River,

which isn't much more than a flash flood river bed. But the way is easy through a small valley. At Jardine Road, turn right (17.3) to cross the river. The road meanders through neat-as-a-pin fields toward San Miguel. Ahead, Highway 101 is glimpsed in the Salinas Valley.

The Estrella Road drops down to meet River Road (23.4) and a spin into San Miguel would be in order with a visit to the mission and a restored adobe, followed by lunch. It is possible to turn left, however, for an eight mile return to Paso Robles.

To go to San Miguel, head north on the two-lane country road along the bluffs above the river. Turn left to San Miguel, crossing the bridge and railroad tracks (24.9). Turn left on Main to the mission, passing a grocery store where supplies may be purchased.

Old Mission San Miguel Arcangel (25.9) was founded in 1797, the 16th in the chain of 21 missions. The interior is reputed to be the best preserved, with original paintings done by the Indians. The courtyard is famous for its cacti, and the cemetery is a quiet oasis full of memories. The museum and gift shop are open 10 a.m. to 5 p.m. daily.

Further south on Mission Street is the Rios-Caledonia Adobe (26.1). To reach the adobe, Y left before going under the 101 Freeway. The structure was built in 1846 and was at one time the Caledonia Inn. It has been restored through the efforts of local enthusiasts and is open from 10 a.m. to 4 p.m. Wednesday through Sunday.

Returning to 14th Street, turn right (27.2), cross the river and turn right on River Road. The road slips along the bluffs and drops down to the river occasionally. The road fords the Estrella River, usually dry here except on a wet day. At Wellsona Road, jog right and left (31.9). Where the bridge crosses over the top of River Road, turn left (35.5) up Experimental Station Road. Climb the steep bank on the rough surface road and turn right on Buena Vista (36.3), and right again on Highway 46 to the start (37.1).

21 ATASCADERO TO PASO ROBLES — WILDFLOWERS FOREVER

Distance: *36 miles*
Loop
Traffic: *light to moderate*
Rating: *moderate to difficult*

The countryside between Atascadero and Paso Robles is sheer delight in spring, a trifle hot in summer, sheer delight in fall, and a trifle cold in winter. On any one day in summer or winter, it can be just right, however. Somewhat removed from the sea breezes and their moderating influences, the area is nonetheless most pleasant.

The ride will go up into the rolling hills between Atascadero and Paso Robles and return partly along the Salinas River, pausing for a moment in Templeton, a tiny town finding restored life in restoration. This could be ridden starting in either Paso Robles or Atascadero. For the purposes of this book, and because this is the way I like to go, the ride will start in Atascadero at the Memorial Building.

From 101 Freeway, take the Highway 41 East off-ramp, and follow 41 (El Camino Real) to the mall in front of the Memorial Building. The Italian Renaissance structure was the head-quarters for the model community call-ed the Atascadero Colony, established in 1913 only to crumble away, leaving the residue that has blossomed into the city of Atascadero, its population now 22,700.

From West Mall Street on Highway 41, head northeast. The street becomes Capistrano Avenue. There is a bike lane through the residential area. Under the railroad bridge, the road becomes Sycamore, caught between the railroad tracks and the bed of the Salinas River. Follow the Highway 41 signs to the Templeton/Creston intersection (2.8). Go straight ahead to Templeton, allow-ing Highway 41 to turn right without you.

The road dips and sways along, through a jumbled land full of little hummocks and little valleys. Turn right on Lupine Lane (5.0), well-named in the spring and early summer, for this is indeed lupine, and poppy, heaven. Fields of poppies, more than are usually seen in these modern days, splash brilliant orange against the green of the grasses.

The hills grow steeper and the road narrower. Farming and ranching on large farms and ranches spread barley, hay and wheat across the curvaceous earth. At El Pomar Drive, turn right (7.6), moving across this rolling, upland area.

Turn left on South El Pomar (9.9), marking the way with red-winged blackbirds, yellow mustard, and total stillness. Turn left on Creston Road (11.4) and Y right, staying on Creston through an area of bogs (*atascadero* means mudhole in Spanish), and drop into the city of Paso Robles. Paso Robles (oak pass) grew originally around natural sulfur hot springs. The springs were developed into a resort in the 1860s. A town grew and the city was incorporated in 1889. Its population is nearing 16,400.

Following the Creston Road through the city, the traffic gets heavy, but just before arriving at the bridge across the river, turn left onto South River Road (17.8). The 170-mile long Salinas River is usually dry by summer, but it has a good flow during wet years through spring. The road does have its ups and downs and will cut up a valley and away into the hills before swinging back to make a right turn on Neal Spring Road (22.1). Arabian horses and eggs are among the crops grown here.

Turn right on El Pomar—sounds familiar, doesn't it?—(23.2), and drop into the little town of Templeton. Don't miss Templeton. In fact, if near lunch

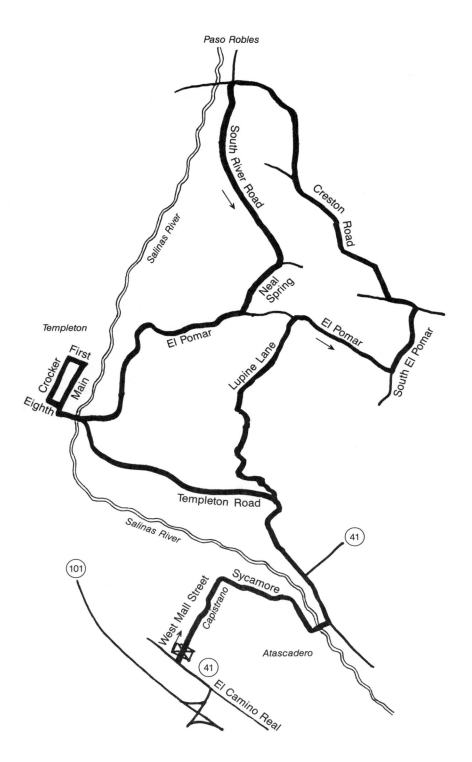

Paso Robles

South River Road

Creston Road

Salinas River

Neal Spring

Templeton

El Pomar

El Pomar

South El Pomar

First

Crocker

Main

Lupine Lane

Eighth

Templeton Road

Salinas River

41

101

West Mall Street

Sycamore

Capistrano

Atascadero

41

El Camino Real

53

time, this is the place to be. Pedal along the river bluff and cross the bridge over the river to turn right on Main Street (26.2). Templeton is dominated by the Templeton Feed and Grain Building, but the interest lies in the restored false-fronted buildings along the main street. Its history starts in 1886 with the coming of the railroad. The business district burned down in 1897. Many of the present buildings have a plaque retelling their histories. There are several cafes, saloons, bars and restaurants to choose from, should a little respite be in order.

Turn left on First Street (26.7) and pedal up one block to Crocker. Turn left again to pass by the Swedish Lutheran Church and at Sixth Street, the Presbyterian Church, both built in 1887. The quiet streets look almost like a movie set. Turn left again on Eighth Street and back to Main (27.7). Turn right on Main and left on Templeton Road to go over the bridge. Keep on the Templeton Road with a right turn (28.3) and head back toward Atascadero.

No shoulder, no traffic and lots of country roller coaster is a good description of the return. At the intersection with Lupine Lane, continue on the Templeton Road (31.0), over a sudden hill, and down along the river and across the bridge. Follow Highway 41 back into Atascadero and the end of the journey (35.9).

22 THE HILLS OF SANTA MARGARITA

Distance: *42 miles*
Loop
Traffic: *light*
Rating: *difficult*

Sometimes in the back country, lonely roads stretch off to surprising places — little towns, half-forgotten, sprawling ranches, whispering creeks, sunny meadows. So it is with this loop, which leaves the little town of Santa Margarita to climb into the La Panza Range, slips so quickly through the town of Pozo that one must be alert to notice it, and then finishes at a new lake with a new focus and new life.

Santa Margarita, on Highway 58, may be reached off Highway 101 between San Luis Obispo and Atascadero. This was the site of Rancho Santa Margarita, an 1841 Mexican land grant rancho, known for years as the queen of the cattle ranches. The town itself, population now 1,100, came into being in 1889 when the Southern Pacific Railroad came through the area.

Start in Santa Margarita where Highway 58 turns east on Estrada, a street named for Joaquin Estrada, the grantee. There is a community park on the corner across the railroad tracks. Turn left on J Street (0.2) and head into the rolling hills. Huge oaks dot the grasslands. At a Y in the road, where Highway 58 goes left, continue to the right (1.5) on the Pozo Road toward Santa Margarita Lake.

At Las Pilitas (4.9), turn left along a narrow, one-and-a-half-lane road to climb up a valley. After a mile, the road tops out on a ridge. The area becomes drier, and the vegetation turns to chaparral. Old and new ranch houses crop up beside the road. The road climbs, sometimes steeply, sometimes gently, with an occasional downhill to rest the legs.

Each valley has its own ranch or settlement, and its uphill. At the Y in the road, keep to the right (11.4) on Pilitas Road to Park Hill Road. The country opens out with wide meadows. There are digger pines and a feeling of the mountains. In the spring, tiny purple flowers dot the pastures. The way becomes more generally downhill after 12 miles (about seven miles of mostly uphill work).

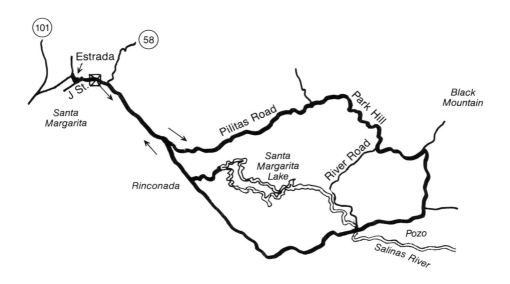

At River Road and Park Hill, continue to the left on the paved road (16.3). Small houses and cabins, farms and ranches are tucked into these valleys. On the top of Black Mountain, to the northwest, are the white globes of the Federal Aviation Administration radar tower. Deer dash across the road and in the spring baby blue-eyes seduce the flower lover.

At about 18 miles there is a steep uphill to move from one meadow to another, like stairsteps. Continue on

Park Hill past the road to the lookout station at Black Mountain (18.8). Black Mountain is in La Panza Range. Interestingly enough, there was a settlement called La Panza at one time back in those hills. La Panza was a gold town, for gold was discovered in 1878 along Placer Creek. There is little or nothing left now but the name.

From here it is downhill toward the town of Pozo. At the intersection with Pozo Road (21.2), continue straight ahead. The road will swing through Pozo (22.6), population about 30, which consists of the U.S. Forest Service station, the library, and the Pozo Saloon. Once a mining town, complete with hotel, it now drowses through the summer days, growing rather lively on Saturday nights at the saloon.

The road is gentle and quiet. River Road, which follows Toro Creek and the headwaters of the 170-mile long Salinas River, comes into Pozo Road (24.3), and then there is a stiff climb for a mile and a half out of the valley to cross a saddle. The vegetation begins to change, growing less dry.

At Rinconada Ghost Town, turn right to go into Santa Margarita Lake (31.8). Pedal up the hill. There is a cafe at the top and the road goes through the entrance (no charge for bicyclists) and down to the marina (33.0). There is a cafe at the marina, and picnic and restroom facilities. The dam was constructed on the Salinas River during World War II to bring water to Camp Roberts. Presently the water is used by the city of San Luis Obispo. The lake itself is a quiet blue shimmer that turns into a hotbed for fishing. Sailing is popular, and the two sports go nicely together, both being of a quiet sort.

Returning up the hill and back to the ghost town, turn right (34.3). A wide, two-lane, gently declining road moves through this wide valley, beside Rinconada Creek, and back into Santa Margarita (42.1).

23 SAN LUIS OBISPO TO MORRO BAY

Distance: *36 miles*
Loop
Traffic: *light to heavy*
Rating: *difficult*
Side trip: *7 miles, difficult*

A fine ride that will start at a California mission, include a side trip to a state beach, pass by a beacon used by mariners for centuries, and let you enjoy a sidewalk seafood cocktail in addition is the loop from San Luis Obispo to Morro Bay. Start early to avoid the afternoon winds, which should blow the bicyclist home after noon.

We will begin at the mission in San Luis Obispo, which can be reached by taking the Broad Street off-ramp from 101 Freeway. Proceed west; the mission is at Broad and Monterey.

Mission San Luis Obispo de Tolosa was founded in 1772, the fifth in the chain of 21 missions. It started as a log cabin but was finally built in the more familiar style after several log structures burned a few times. During its era of disrepair, it went through a New England-style period with clapboard siding and a shake roof. Restoration, however, has returned it to adobe and tile. There is a museum which has as one of its most famous objects a vestment worn by Father Serra. It is open from 9 a.m. to 4 p.m. daily.

There are several interesting, historical buildings in the area, including, at the corner of Chorro and Palm, the Ah Louis Store, a State Historical Landmark. Built in 1874, it was the first Chinese store in the county and served as a general store, bank, counting house and post office for the Chinese who dug the eight tunnels for Southern Pacific through the Cuesta Mountains north of the city.

From Broad and Monterey, head south on Broad to Higuera Street and turn right (0.1). This is the main street of San Luis Obispo, but there is a bike lane to follow through the congested area and into the southern, more industrialized part of town.

Y to the right at Madonna Road (1.1) and cross over the 101 Freeway on the bike lane. Pedal by Laguna Lake Park and turn right at Los Osos Valley Road (2.5). The bike lane continues through this newer section of San Luis Obispo. As the road moves out of town, on the right is one of the "Nine Sisters," a line of volcanic plugs that stride their way to the sea, the last being Morro Rock. They are old, old, old—50 million years old. The peak on the immediate right is Cerro San Luis, with an elevation of 1,292, and farther west is Bishop Peak, 1,559 feet.

The wide Los Osos Valley makes for pleasant spinning, and with an early start, you can avoid the brisk afternoon breeze.

A sign, "Welcome to the Valley of the Bears," brings one to the little town of Los Osos (the bears). The area's history begins with a camp by the Portola Expedition in 1769. It was named for the California grizzlies in the area. Continue through the town of Los Osos to the Pecho Valley Road (12.6).

For the sidetrip to Montana de Oro, turn left (south) on Pecho Road. To continue on the main ride, turn north on Pecho Road toward the golf course for a ride through Cuesta by the Sea, a little community founded in the 1920s. Turn right on Binscarth (13.0) and left on Fearn Avenue (13.3) as the streets work their way through the often fog-shrouded town overlooking Morro Bay's estuary.

The estuary is home for 80 percent of all sea life along the Central Coast. The bay is a nutrient trap for plant and animal life and acts as a spawning ground and nursery for fish and fowl. It abounds in wildlife, much hidden from the casual observer. A pair of binoculars would be in order to catch the merest glimpse into this ecological paradise.

Fearn turns right onto Ramona to

SIDE TRIP: *7 miles*

MONTANA DE ORO

The 7,000-acre state beach is named, it is said, Mountain of Gold for the California poppies, fiddleneck, wild mustard and bush monkey flowers that bloom in spring over its gentle slopes. You will not think the slopes all that gentle, for it will be a pull up a narrow road to the left for one mile, with views north toward Morro Rock along the wide sweep of Estero Bay. Then there is a swift drop through a forest of eucalyptus for almost two miles, where the road levels before dropping down to a cove (3.4). Here the waves roar in and break in gnashing rhythm. The day I was there the Purple Sailing Jellyfish, a jellyfish of the high seas, had washed ashore, after some catastrophe, by the hundred thousands. Heaped in royal blue bands where the waves had deposited them, they coated the sands, a strange display of the sea.

The road continues on two more miles and there are camping, picnic and restroom facilities, but we will return, pumping up the hill and gliding back to Los Osos. At the turn onto Los Osos Valley Road, continue straight ahead on Pecho Road (6.8).

Baywood Park. Baywood Park is the third of the communities perched out on the south side of Morro Bay. It dates from 1919. Turn left on Fourth Street (13.9) and right on Santa Ysabel Avenue (14.5) through this residential area.

At the signal, which is South Bay Boulevard, turn left toward Morro Bay (15.4). The road moves along the shoulder of the estuary with good views of the bay and Morro Bay State Park. Turn left to go to Morro Bay State Park (17.1), riding along the base of Black Mountain past the campground entrance and the golf course. The road is now Country Club Drive, which goes into the town of Morro Bay. On the left is the boat channel and marina and on the right cypress and homes climbing the hill.

The road becomes Main Street. At Olive turn left to Morro Avenue. At Marina Street, turn left (19.7) and then right onto The Embarcadero. Restaurants and seafood stores crowd along the way. Ahead is Morro Rock and the Pacific Gas and Electric Morro Bay Power Plant. Follow The Embarcadero out to Morro Rock (21.2).

The rock stands 578 feet (or 576 or 581, depending on the source of information). It was described by Cabrillo in 1542. The word *morro* means rock, so it is a Rock Rock of uncommon stature. On the top is a nesting area for the rare peregrine falcon, and climbing the rock is forbidden. It is sometimes called "The Gibraltar of the Pacific."

The seas push hard against the mouth of the bay, and on a rough day, watching any boats trying to make their way out is certainly interesting and makes one happy to stay aboard a bicycle rather than take up the sea. Be sure to cross the spit (if the bicycle can stand the rutted parking lot) to view the combers that flash ashore at Atascadero State Beach. There is a sheltered picnic area here.

Return along The Embarcadero and turn left on Beach Street (22.5), up a short, steep hill. Turn right on Monterey (22.7) and left on Dunes to Quintana Road (23.0).

Turn right for a return to San Luis Obispo. Follow Quintana until it deadends at Highway 1 (25.3). With the wind at your back you will blow by Cuesta College and Camp San Luis Obispo before the road slides up a hill and then dips down into San Luis Obispo. Cal Poly (California Polytechnic State University) is on the left. Once into town, Highway 1 becomes Santa Rosa Street. Cross the freeway and pedal up the hill to turn right at Palm Street (35.5) and return to the mission area (35.8).

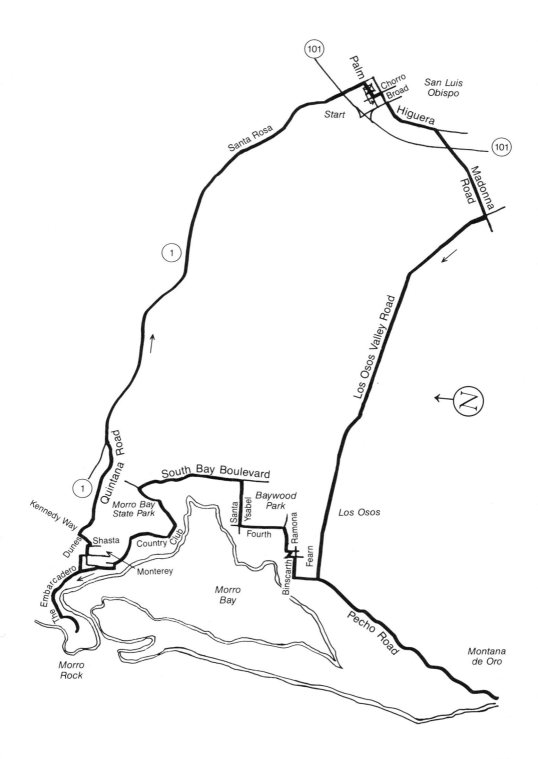

24 SANTA MARGARITA LAKE

Distance: *35 miles*
Semi-loop
Traffic: *moderate to heavy (in town)*
Rating: *moderate*

Santa Margarita Lake is one of those quiet backwaters that have sprung up in this semiarid area with the invention of dams. For all its man-made aspect, the lake looks perfect, quite as though it were dropped here by the hand of erosion rather than the hand of man. The mountains surrounding it look down with equanimity on the sky-blue glitter in their midst. And it makes a pleasant destination from the town of Atasca-

dero, which was founded in 1913 as Atascadero Colony, a model community. The name *Atascadero* means mudhole in Spanish, and there are many marshes tucked here and there among the low rolling hills of this town bordering the Salinas River.

The ride will start at the Atascadero Memorial Building mall, reached from 101 Freeway by taking the Highway 41 East off-ramp. The mall is at the corner of El Camino Real (the main street) and Highway 41 (between the streets of East and West Mall). The Memorial Building is the imposing Italian Renaissance revival in Andrea Palladio-style at the head of the mall. It was built in 1914 and served as headquarters for the colony.

From the mall, follow Highway 41 west by turning left onto El Camino Real and right (0.3) on Highway 41 to go under 101 Freeway onto Old Morro Road. The traffic goes from heavy to moderate to light. Turn left onto Atascadero Avenue (0.7). This two-lane road with a marked shoulder winds back and forth and up and down through the low rolling hills of Atascadero. Homes spread about on the

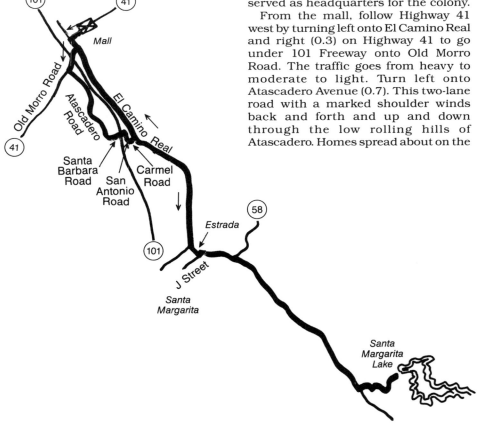

countryside through a residential area.

Atascadero Road becomes Santa Barbara Road (3.9) and crosses back over 101 Freeway. At San Antonio Road (4.2), turn right, paralleling the freeway and then swinging away east over low hills. Turn left at Carmel (5.9) and right onto El Camino Real (6.2). Oats, barley, and orchards watch the passing bicyclist along the flat valley floor.

At the sign to Santa Margarita Lake, Highway 58, turn left (9.2) to cross the railroad tracks on Estrada, named for the grantee who received the Mexican land grant rancho, Santa Margarita, in 1841. The tiny town has been a cattle-raising center for years. At the edge of town, turn left, following Highway 58, on J Street (9.4). The road swings up through low rolling hills and into a wide valley. At the Y, continue to the right (10.7) toward Santa Margarita Lake. The road goes through a valley one ridge over from the Salinas River's outflow from the dam.

At the left turn to Santa Margarita Lake (17.1) is Rinconada Ghost Town. Pedal up the hill past the cafe to the entrance gate. There is no fee for bicyclists. A swoop down to lakeside (18.4) will reveal a picnic area and a cafe. The lake is day use only. There is no swimming allowed in the lake, but there is a swimming pool. Still, a quiet stroll at lakeside, watching the fishermen plying their avocation, is reward enough for the pleasant ride.

Returning, turn right at the ghost town and follow Highway 58 into Santa Margarita (27.5). The center of town is to the left should you want to pedal about, enjoying the views. Heading north out of town, follow El Camino Real straight into Atascadero. Turn right on Highway 41, East Mall, to return to the start (35.4).

25 CANYONS TO THE SEA

Distance: *39 miles*
Loop
Traffic: *Light to heavy*
Rating: *moderate to difficult*

Quiet backcountry roads, the lazy circles hawks make in the sky, old oaks and sunny open fields, old towns, the crash of the surf and the smell of salt water taffy form the nucleus for this ride that seems to encompass what the Central Coast and bicycling are all about. It is best to leave early to avoid the pesky afternoon winds that defeat headway northward. The route will begin in Arroyo Grande, swing through Grover City, up into the rolling hills toward San Luis Obispo, down to the sea at Avila Beach, and then return via the Pismo clams' home base.

Arroyo Grande High School is the starting place. It may be reached from Freeway 101 — from the north take Halcyon Road south to Fair Oaks Avenue and turn left to Valley Road; from the south take Traffic Way north to Fair Oaks and turn left to Valley Road.

Leaping on the bicycle, pedal west on Fair Oaks through this oldest town in southern San Luis Obispo County, being founded in 1862. Turn right on South Elm Street (1.2) and left at the signal on Grand Avenue (1.8). This is the main street in Arroyo Grande and Grover City, four lanes and busy. Turn right upon entering Grover City on Oak Park Boulevard (2.2) and climb the hill for less than half a mile. Grover City was founded in 1890 by Mr. Grover — it is a mere stripling of a town. After cresting the hill, race down and out of town across 101 Freeway. New condominiums spread across the hills, eating at the land.

Turn left on Old Oak Park (3.8). The road narrows to a lane and a half and climbs up a shallow canyon. The pull gets steeper and huge big homes hang on the hills. Turn left onto Ormonde Road (5.6) and look back toward Santa Maria and the whole sweep of the coast. The road tops out at six miles and plunges downhill through eucalyptus groves to Price Canyon. The sound and smell of oil drilling and pumping cut the air. The road drops under the railroad (7.4). Watch for traffic going through the subway, for there is not room for a bicyclist and a motor vehicle together. There is truck traffic on the road, so it behooves one to listen before entering the passage. Pull up out of the defile, over Corral de Piedra Creek, and turn right onto Price Canyon Road (7.7).

The road is a wide two-lane with a marked shoulder, steadily rising from the sea into the back canyons. At the intersection with Highway 227, turn left toward San Luis Obispo (9.3). This is the open Luis Valley, the "high way" to San Luis Obispo through a little town now semideceased, Edna.

Turn left on Buckley Road (12.0), pedal by the County Airport, still in the open, rather flat land, heavily farmed. Buckley becomes Vachell. At South Higuera Street (15.0), turn left, following the old cement highway and pass under 101 Freeway (16.7). Bear right onto the Pacific Coast Bicentennial Route, at this point Ontario Road (16.8), which parallels the freeway.

Continuing on Ontario Road, cross San Luis Bay Road and the bridge and turn right on Avila Beach (19.0). The road winds through a steep-sided canyon thick with chaparral and oaks. The road is two-lane and busy, but well populated with bicyclists and with a relatively decent shoulder. It slips by the San Luis Bay Golf Course, through which San Luis Obispo Creek gurgles. Continue past Avila Beach for a visit to Port San Luis (24.0).

The port has an interesting history. It was developed in 1860 and for a time served as a deep water port for the narrow gauge railroad, loading and unloading passengers and products. There was a motel here, built in 1884,

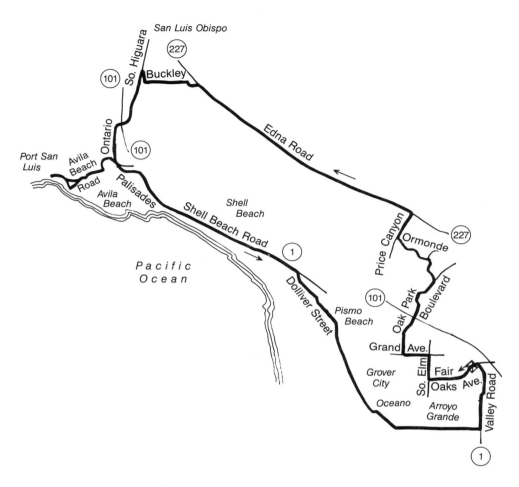

which later burned. There was also a whaling station. But activity slowed around the turn of the century, not to be revived until the 1950s. It is now a major commercial fishing port, accounting for one-third of all albacore taken in California waters in the early 1970s. There is a restaurant, the Old Port Inn, on the wharf, and a cafe at the entrance.

Returning to Avila Beach, turn right on Front Street (25.4) where there are cafes along the waterfront. Avila Beach and Port San Luis are sheltered from the winds and surprisingly warm. Avila attracts the college crowd from Cal Poly

almost all year long. Sometimes it seems that while every other area in the vicinity is shrouded in fog, Avila is sunny.

Turn left on San Luis Street (25.7) and pull up the hill through the residential area and then down to join Avila Road and head back inland. Before reaching the 101 Freeway on-ramp, turn right on Palisades Road (28.3). The road climbs over a low ridge and then drops into Shell Beach. The little town was non-existent, nothing but fields of peas, until 1926, when a developer bought the pea fields and laid out lots.

Shell Beach Road continues on into

Pismo Beach. Y right onto Dolliver Street (32.4), which has a bike lane. Pismo Beach was founded in 1891 and at one time was a mecca for tourists enjoying the cool, foggy weather, the famed Pismo clams and the wide sandy beaches.

Follow Dolliver, which is just inland from Pismo Beach State Park, with access to the beach, through Grover City. The road is pleasant as it swings down into Oceano, another little town which has seen better days. Advancing sand dunes destroyed its famed dance pavilion years ago. Follow Highway 1 (Cienaga) out of town, across the flat fields to the hill and turn left on Valley Road (37.9). The Victorian house on the right is one of several in the area, and was built in 1886. Follow Valley Road to Fair Oaks and the high school parking lot (39.2).

26 LOPEZ LAKE AND THE FIVE CITIES AREA

Distance: *37 miles*
Semi-loop
Traffic: *light to moderate*
Rating: *easy to moderate*
Easier variation: *out and back,*
  22 miles

This ride is so pleasant that the tendency is to keep going on and on. Lopez Lake is the destination. A ride from Arroyo Grande to the Lake and return [about 22 miles of fairly easy going) is a delight in itself, but adding a swing through the Luis Valley and then down along the seashore is the cream in the Oreo cookie, the frosting on the cake.

The problem with the ride is not the land, which is beautiful; or the weather, which in all probability will be cool summer and winter; but the wind. It zings up this valley, if it is blowing at all, by noon. So a lovely ride heading east in the morning may be repaid, if one lingers at the lake, with a good westerly in the afternoon. But of course, in late fall, winter and early spring, it may not come up at all. And one way or another, calm or blowing, the lake is a beautiful destination, cradled in Lopez Canyon's dark green walls, a blue diamond in the sun.

The starting point will be in Arroyo Grande at Arroyo Grande High School, reached off 101 Freeway from the north by taking Halcyon south to Fair Oaks and turning left to Valley Road; and from the south by taking Traffic Way north to Fair Oaks and turning left to Valley Road.

From the high school parking lot proceed east on Fair Oaks Avenue to Traffic Way, turn left (0.3). At the Y in the street, bear right on Bridge Street to the parking lot just over the creek. Turn right to pedal through Arroyo Grande's Village Green. Paths lead down to Arroyo Grande Creek below, a quiet place full of leafy smells.

Turn left on Short Street and right on West Branch, through the business district. At the juncture with Highway 227 (1.2), take Huasna Road toward Lopez Lake, which is the Y right. Almost immediately the way is out of town through an area of small acreages—everyone having two head of cattle and two head of horses.

The road moves ever so gently uphill along the arroyo dug by Arroyo Grande Creek. Sycamores and oaks crowd along the creek, but the hills are grassy. The road begins to steepen somewhat to come up the dam (8.3), where the lake sparkles its blue jewels under a blue sky. The road moves along the south side of the lake to the entrance to the park (10.9). There is no charge for bicyclists. There is a picnic area just to the left beyond the entrance, or one may pedal up a low ridge and drop down to the marina, where a store and cafe are located. There is overnight camping available. The end of the road (11.8) is just beyond the marina. The lake and recreation area opened in 1969. The picnic area and the shore are heavy in oaks. Add 2 miles to go into the lake.

Returning from the lake, go straight back to Arroyo Grande for the easy variation, or turn right at Orcutt Road (18.1) for a ride through the upland valleys east of Arroyo Grande. Here the traffic is light and the way straight (more or less). After passing through a marshy area the road climbs out to the open Luis Valley. Huge new homes dot the uplands. One expects Mercedes and Cadillacs and Corvettes; one usually sees pickup trucks.

At Biddle Ranch Road (23.1), turn left to cross the valley, and then left again at Highway 227 (24.2). The highway is a broad, two-lane road with a wide shoulder. Turn right on Price Canyon Road (25.4) along a two-lane road that goes into the Pismo Creek oil fields. The smell is heavy with oil, and the roar of the machinery will take the sound of the wind out of your ears.

As the road comes into Pismo Beach, houses hang on the side of the cliffs above. Price Canyon Road crosses 101

65

Freeway and becomes Hinds Avenue. Continue straight ahead to the Pismo Pier for a walk on the wild surf side (30.4). From the pier, there is a beautiful view south along San Luis Obispo Bay on a clear day to Point Sal south of Santa Maria. The pier has the look of the 1920s, battered by time and the elements. From the 1890s through the 1920s the area turned into a tent city each summer as residents of the hot San Joaquin Valley flocked westward to enjoy the summer fog. A large dance pavilion, located where the pier touches the shore, was the center of activity.

Returning on Hinds, turn right on Dolliver Street (30.5) on a bike lane. Pismo was founded in 1895 and was famed for years for the Pismo clams. Clamming is on the wane, however, and now the Pismo dunes at Pismo Beach State Park attract campers and dune-buggies.

Traffic can be heavy through the downtown. The route, which becomes Highway 1, swings through Grover City, keeping along the beach front parks. Follow Highway 1, entering Oceano, a town that at one time was a prime resort area. Back in 1904, the town had a dance pavilion, a wharf and beach cottages, all now lost to the advancing sand dunes.

On the right is the Oceano Depot, slated to be a museum, and built in 1896. Also, just before leaving town, on the left is a huge Victorian mansion with a cluster of little trailers huddled at its foundation. Built in 1885 by Coffee T. Rice, it is in the process of being restored.

The highway leads out of town across the flat Arroyo Grande Creek plain. Cross the plain to the hill and turn left (35.4) on Valley Road. Another Victorian is on the right as you enter town. This is the Parker-Davis home, built in 1886. It was restored in 1957–59 and served as a restaurant for a time. It is now a private residence.

The road will continue until it meets Fair Oaks Avenue and the high school (36.7). Turn right to the parking lot (36.8).

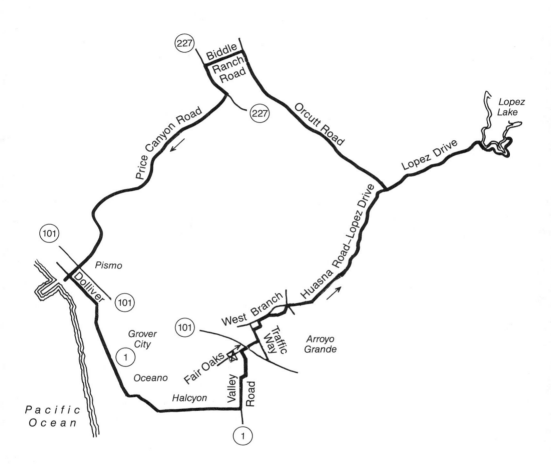

27 THE HUASNA VALLEY

Distance: *31 miles*
Semi-loop
Traffic: *light to moderate*
Rating: *moderate to difficult*
Side trip: *5 miles, difficult*
Easy variation: *Out and back, 20 miles*

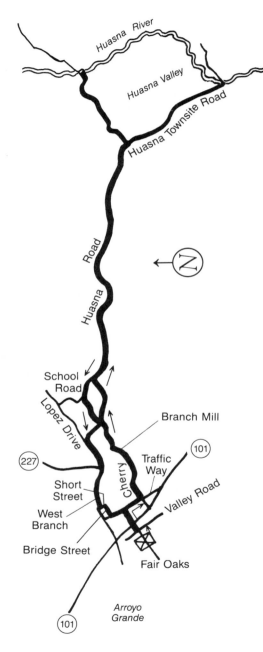

The Huasna Valley is supposed to be, say those who know, the stairway, the ladder, to the heavens. That is what the Chumash were said to believe, although all the Chumash have ascended the ladder and can no longer speak for their legends.

But the Huasna Valley will turn out to be a sunny spot tucked back in the hills west of Arroyo Grande. The Chumash village once called Wasna is long gone, as is the 27,000-acre Spanish land grant Rancho Huasna. What is there is a surprising gathering of small and large farms and a one-room schoolhouse built in 1907, no longer in use. A short, easy trip out the Huasna Road to the steeper part would be pleasant without going into the valley. It would be about 20 miles.

The ride will start at Arroyo Grande High School, reached from the south on 101 Freeway by the first Arroyo Grande off-ramp onto Traffic Way with a left turn onto Fair Oaks Avenue. The high school is at the corner of Fair Oaks and Valley Road. From the north on 101 Freeway, take the Halcyon Road off-ramp south to Fair Oaks Avenue and turn left to Valley Road.

From the high school, proceed east on Fair Oaks Avenue, across the freeway to Traffic Way. Turn right (0.3), ride two blocks to East Cherry Avenue and turn left (0.4) along a residential drive. *Arroyo grande* means big ditch or gulch. The town was founded in 1862 and has been enjoying a steady renaissance in the last few years. Population is now over 14,000.

East Cherry Avenue becomes Branch Mill Road with a right turn (0.9) and, presto, you are across the fields, out of town and riding along the base of the arroyo with the hill to the right very steep and covered thickly with chaparral, and the fields, open and sunny, to the left. At Huasna Road, turn right (3.0). The road winds and climbs through the rolling hills past ranches and farms. The open canyon begins to pinch in as sycamores and oaks shade the road. The road moves gradually uphill and as it does, the valley opens out again to fields, in the spring, of lupine and mustard and fiddleneck — blues and yellows and oranges.

On the left is Tar Spring Ridge and on the right Newsom Ridge. After 10 miles the road begins a two-mile climb. It crests and drops steeply downhill into the Huasna Valley.

Just when it appears that there is no civilization (except fences) left on the face of the earth, ranches appear and then a sign proclaims "Welcome to the Huasna Valley — population 171," a greeting from the Huasna Valley 4-H Club (12.6).

Turn south on the Huasna Townsite Road and ride past the little red schoolhouse on the right. Beyond the apple orchard the road runs through a sunny, open area, meandering along one side of the Huasna Valley. Farms and ranches dot the landscape. Cattle, horses and sheep nibble on the grasses. The road begins to slide down to the river, turning to a dirt lane just before arriving at a bridge (15.5) over the river.

The return will be back to the Huasna Road and a left turn (18.5). There will be a one-mile uphill and then the long downhill.

At the spot where Huasna Road turns left, go straight ahead (26.8) on School Road for a variation. The road climbs suddenly for a short period, past a school, and becomes Branch Mill (go straight ahead). Turn right on Huasna Road (28.2) and go across the fields and turn left on Lopez Drive (28.7) toward town.

Here the traffic count will pick up. Turn left onto Highway 227 (30.2) after entering Arroyo Grande and pedal along Branch Street. Just past the city hall, on the left, is Short Street (30.7), which leads down to the Village Green and the Swinging Bridge. Turn left to the green.

SIDE TRIP: *5 miles*

TO THE HUASNA RIVER

There is a choice that can be made at the Huasna sign — to go straight ahead or turn right. A right turn, which is the main trip, leads into the Huasna Valley itself. By going straight ahead, a side trip up a canyon and down to the Huasna River before the road goes to dirt makes for a challenging addition.

Continuing straight ahead from the intersection the road passes by an apple orchard and becomes narrow and windy. It turns uphill after half a mile and climbs a half mile steeply. At the cattle guard views north and east are of the Santa Lucia Range and into Los Padres National Forest.

There is a steep and fast downhill on the very narrow road. In the spring this is a wildflower haven. At the bridge where the pavement ends is the Huasna River, which goes dry in the summer and fall. The distance from the intersection to the bridge is two and a half miles. A return pump up the steep hill and a glide down to the intersection at the Huasna School totals 4.8 miles.

The "back side" of the main street has become a pleasant park with a large parking lot. There are trails down to the river, and a green glen with quiet waters. At the corner of the parking lot and Bridge Street is a bicycle shop and to the north, across Branch Street, is an ice cream store that seems to always have a line of customers outside, hot or cold weather. Across the bridge is the South County Historical Society Museum.

From the Village Green, go south, to the left, on Bridge Street to Traffic Way and then turn right on Fair Oaks (30.9) and return to the high school parking lot (31.2).

28 NIPOMO MESA

Distance: *19 miles*
Loop
Traffic: *light to moderate*
Rating: *easy to moderate*

The community of Nipomo (meaning "at the foot of the hills") sprawls across the Nipomo Valley and on the mesas on either side. It looks to be a settlement of perhaps 1,000 people, but the population is close to 10,000, for people are sprinkled and spread over an area much larger than supposed.

Indians were the first to settle along Nipomo Creek almost 9,000 years ago. The town was named in 1830, and its most famous pioneer was Captain William Goodwin Dana, the cousin of Richard Henry Dana, author of *Two Years Before the Mast*. The town experienced a railroad boom in the 1880s when the narrow gauge Pacific Coast Railway went through. A depot, warehouse and loading platform were built and the town grew rapidly. An 1888 fire destroyed most of the downtown, however, and it is now a quiet, rural community of open vistas and shady, tree-lined roads, just right for bicycling.

A pleasant ride through Nipomo will start just north of Santa Maria and south of Nipomo at the intersection of Highway 101 and Highway 166.

Head north on Thompson Road toward Nipomo. The road is two-lane, rather wide. It breaks away from 101 immediately, and moves gradually up onto the mesa where the views are of rolling hills, old barns and cattle. At three and a half miles the town of Nipomo appears with the large new Saint Joseph's Catholic Church dominating the scene. In the middle of town, on the right, is the old white church building that presently houses an antique shop. It was built in the 1880s. Across the street is Jocko's, open for lunch with the motto: "Come in an monkey round." It is a popular local

watering hole.

Continuing north out of Nipomo, the flat mesa makes for easy riding with only an occasional pull. The road makes a wide sweeping turn and ducks under Highway 101 (7.1) to emerge as Los Berros Road. It wanders through a rolling valley shaded with eucalyptus. Turn left on Pomeroy Road toward the golf course (8.7) through an area with new small homes. There is a good-sized pimple on the landscape that must be climbed onto an upland. Eggs are for sale, along with goats and ponies and rabbits and

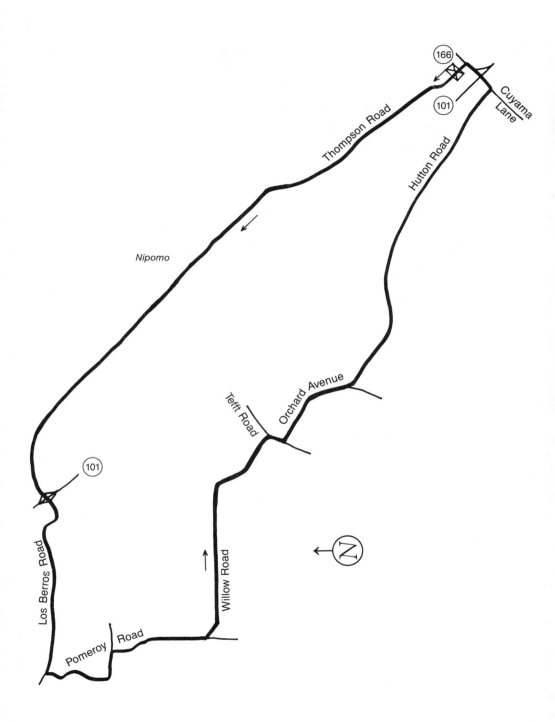

166

101

Cuyama
Lane

Thompson Road

Hutton Road

Nipomo

Orchard Avenue

Tefft Road

101

Los Berros Road

Willow Road

Pomeroy Road

N

strawberries, all the things that go with the kind of small acreage prevalent in the area. The road roller coasters along. Turn right on Tefft Road (13.7). On the corner is the Nipomo Regional County Park, which has picnic and restroom facilities, plus baseball diamonds. Almost immediately, turn left onto Orchard Avenue, a road shaded by eucalyptus. Orchard Y's to the left (14.6) and continues south along a narrow roadway with moderate traffic.

Suddenly the road breaks out of the trees and into an open, sagebrush-covered area. Under crackling power lines and tower, the road bends and becomes Hutton Road, paralleling 101. Past the Santa Maria Speedway, pedal to the intersection with Cuyama Lane (18.5) and turn left to Thompson to go under the freeway and return to the starting point (18.6).

29 OSO FLACO LAKE

Distance: *35 miles*
Semi-loop
Traffic: *moderate*
Rating: *easy*

A blue sparkling lake and velvet gold sand dunes await the bicyclist at the end of a ride from Santa Maria to Oso Flaco Lake. Oso Flaco, by the way, means "skinny bear." There must be a story there. Actually, there is. Members of the Portola expedition named the lake in 1769 when they killed a lean bear and had him for dinner. The winds come up early in Santa Maria, so all westward ranging should be completed by 11 a.m. to 12 noon. Returning east is always a breeze.

The starting point will be Waller Park in Santa Maria, which can be reached off Highway 101 by taking the Betteravia Road off-ramp, west, to Highway 135 (Broadway) and turning left, or south. The park is a delightful oasis of green lawns, cool pines and cedars, duck ponds and picnic areas. From the park head north on Highway 135 on the wide shoulder and through the center of Santa Maria's downtown. The historical society museum is on the right (3.0) and it is worth a visit.

The city came about through the Homestead Law, which resulted in Civil War veterans being given free land. The winds roared unimpeded through the valley from the sea, and the new plantings of those first farmers were blown away. However, eucalyptus windbreaks were planted in 1875 and the fine soil began to yield some of the crops that now cause this area to be called "The Valley of Gardens." Broadway is the main street and made wide enough to allow a farm wagon and team to turn around without having to go around the block. The name of the new town was Central City until the Post Office said differently. It seems there was a Central City in Colorado, and the mail kept getting mixed up.

Turn left at Main Street (3.2), which is Highway 166, another wide street. At the juncture of Main and Broadway is the Santa Maria Town Center, which replaced a derelict downtown in the 1970s. After a half mile the city traffic thins out and the outskirts of town appear. The road becomes three-lane, then two, with a marked shoulder.

The land is very flat and pedaling is easy. Classic old two-story farmhouses punctuate the sweep of the land. Crops are grown on every side, as far as the eye can see, to the hills rimming the horizon. Straight ahead is the only break — the sea.

The town of Guadalupe has a population of 5,600 and was at one time the major settlement in the valley. The narrow gauge Pacific Railroad, however, went through Central City instead of Guadalupe, and with it went Guadalupe's businesses. Later Southern Pacific went through Guadalupe, but the damage had been done. Guadalupe gained a wild west reputation, which it still has.

Turn right onto Highway 1 (10.9). There is a bike lane through Guadalupe. The Far Western Restaurant may, even in the morning, smell of the barbecued steaks that are so famous in the region. There is a county park, Leroy, just on the edge of town, along the Santa Maria River. Cross the river and continue north. The highway is a wide two-lane road with a marked shoulder.

The land continues to be billiard table flat. Turn left on Oso Flaco Lake Road (14.6). The road leads toward the dunes through broccoli fields and comes into an area bordered by lakes like blue jewels tucked into the dunes (17.8). The lakes attract fishermen and sunbathers. Beyond the dunes is the sea, rolling long blue combers against the golden sand. The area is a clam preserve that stretches from Oceano on the north to the mouth of the Santa Maria delta.

Returning from the lakes, continue on

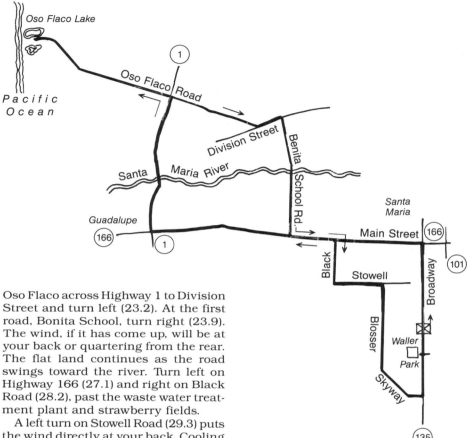

Oso Flaco across Highway 1 to Division Street and turn left (23.2). At the first road, Bonita School, turn right (23.9). The wind, if it has come up, will be at your back or quartering from the rear. The flat land continues as the road swings toward the river. Turn left on Highway 166 (27.1) and right on Black Road (28.2), past the waste water treatment plant and strawberry fields.

A left turn on Stowell Road (29.3) puts the wind directly at your back. Cooling sheds for crops, frozen food companies and other food processors line the road. Turn right on Blosser Road (31.3). There is a bike lane. Blosser becomes Skyway Drive. The road curves around to meet the 135 Expressway. Turn left (34.7) and return to Waller Park (35.5).

30 TEPUSQUET AND TWITCHELL PANT AND PUFF

Distance: *42 miles*
Loop
Traffic: *light*
Rating: *difficult*

The building of Twitchell Dam brought to an end for the residents of the Santa Maria Valley the fear of flooding from the Cuyama River. The river bed is actually higher than the valley itself, and when a wet year occurred (not often), there was a sense of doom that settled over the fertile fields. The Cuyama River and the Sisquoc River join in the upper end of the Santa Maria Valley to make the Santa Maria River. The Cuyama comes from far up the Cuyama Valley, carrying excess water from the somber, almost nude hills of that area. Water from the lake behind the dam is used for irrigation. It is only rarely that the lake fills, and there is no recreational use, more's the pity.

Tepusquet is not much more than a canyon that spills out of the San Rafael Mountains. It is named for the Mexican land grant Rancho Tepusquet, a holding of 8,900 acres granted in 1838. The road winds up Buckhorn Canyon to the ridge top and plunges down Tepusquet to Santa Maria. There are marvelous views from up on the ridge, and this ride will both tax and delight the bicycle pedaler. The climb is about 1,200 feet in three miles, which is no joke.

The starting point will be north and east of Santa Maria, three miles east of Highway 101 on Highway 166 at the Bull Canyon intersection. It may be reached by turning east on Highway 166 from 101. Highway 166 is the road to Maricopa and Bakersfield. By starting at Bull Canyon, we will avoid the 101 Freeway.

The highway moves through the grassy hills with a gentle gradient up and down. Oaks. sycamores and cottonwoods grow in the canyons, and as the road climbs, the oaks climb the sides of the hills. Off the top of the first big climb the San Rafael Range looms ahead. The first indication of the lake behind Twitchell will show on the right. There is a long, curved white bridge that takes the road across the Huasna River, and if the lake is down (as it usually is), it will be hard to picture the fact that the lake can extend under the bridge and up the Huasna Valley some six miles.

At the bridge across Alamo Creek (5.4), looking down onto the lake bed, the old road and its bridges can be glimpsed if the water level is low. Steep-sided hills plunge into the valley. Often the light is brilliant in the area because of the afternoon winds. The greens of the hills seem to glow.

Turn right on the road to Tepusquet (11.7) and pedal along Buckhorn Canyon. A tiny settlement includes humans, goats, horses and cows in the population. The road winds through a narrow valley shaded with sycamores and oaks and begins an upward climb after about two miles. Ceanothus in bloom crowd downward over the road during the spring. The climb becomes unrelenting, the hill steeper and steeper. The view spirals down and down, across ridges and peaks far to the east, and the road is no more than one and a half lanes wide. Just when you might think there is no civilization left on the world, there is a school bus stop near the crest (16.7). Now begins the fun. But watch for cattle in the road on this long downhill of six miles.

This area is famous for its flagstone, sliced from the strata that is occasionally exposed in road-cuts. A farmhouse shows that civilization is near. Now houses come thick and fast along Tepusquet Creek. The way is shady and the air thick with the smells of damp ferny dells.

Slowly the steep downhill becomes shallow and the canyon widens out to meet the wide Santa Maria Valley.

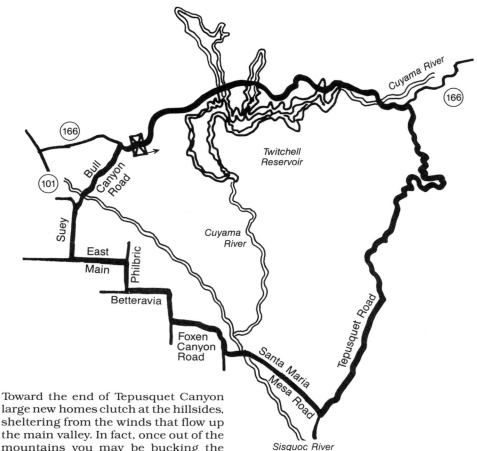

Toward the end of Tepusquet Canyon large new homes clutch at the hillsides, sheltering from the winds that flow up the main valley. In fact, once out of the mountains you may be bucking the winds yourself. If you are lucky, the winds will be a brisk breeze, or even, wonder of wonders, no wind at all.

At a Y in the road, turn right onto Santa Maria Mesa Road (26.1) and climb a sudden bluff onto a flat area planted heavily to vineyards. The Sisquoc River is to the left. Ahead is the Santa Maria Valley and nothing but the sea. The only thing on the horizon might be a bank of fog or the tail end of storm clouds. Cross the river (29.8) and bear right on Foxen Canyon Road (30.5). The road runs across billiard table flat fields in a series of rights and lefts. A wide, sweeping left puts you on Betteravia. Turn right on Philbric (34.7) and left on East Main (36.2). Arriving at the outskirts of Santa Maria, turn right on Suey Road (38.4).

The road will Y right (39.1) onto what becomes Bull Canyon Road. The road crosses the Santa Maria River and starts up a little canyon through an area of small ranches with cattle and horses. The road winds up the sycamore-shaded Suey Creek with an occasional steep pitch to the Cuyama Highway and the beginning of the trek (42.0).

31 GUADALUPE SAND DUNES

Distance: *33 miles*
Semi-loop
Traffic: *moderate*
Rating: *easy*

The Guadalupe sand dunes are part of a long shoreline at the mouth of the Santa Maria River that is a result of both the work of the sea and the persistent winds that blow inland. At one time the Santa Maria Valley could not grow crops because of the wind, which simply dug the new crops up and hurled them downwind. It was only after planting eucalyptus in windbreaks that "The Valley of Gardens" became anything more than a desert.

This is a most pleasant and easy ride if the westward leg is taken early enough to avoid the afternoon winds. An early start, followed by a late return, means no headwinds on the way out and a good push on the way back. The starting point in Santa Maria will be Waller Park, located off Highway 135

south of Betteravia Road. From Highway 101 take the Betteravia Road off-ramp to 135 and turn left to the park.

Waller is a delightful area with a beautiful stand of pines and cedars, pools, picnic areas and a rolling carpet of green grass. From the park pedal north on Highway 135 (Broadway). It is a four-lane, busy city street, but once a turn is made, to the left on Betteravia Road (1.1), the traffic begins to thin out and you will be propelled into the countryside.

The road Y's just out of town. Go right, staying on Betteravia Road. There is a marked bike path along the road, indicating there may have been other bicyclists before you. You are not a pioneer.

Cattle graze the flat pastures. The large Holly sugar plant gobbles sugar beets. The fertilizer company clears the sinuses.

Betteravia turns into Simas Street. At Highway 166, turn left (9.4) and con-

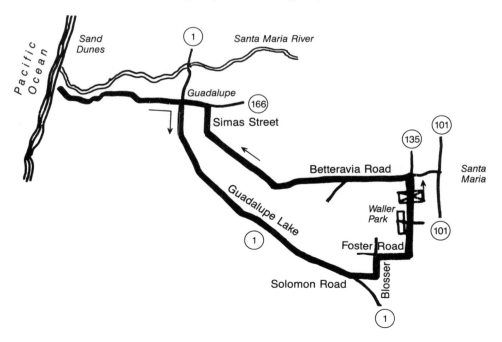

tinue into the town of Guadalupe. The town was settled in the 1860s and the stagecoach came through Guadalupe beginning in 1873. But in 1882 the businessmen packed up and moved to Central City, the early name of Santa Maria. Population of the town is now 5,600.

Continue on through Guadalupe, past the cemetery and toward the sand dunes that have been used by film-makers to depict the dunes of the Sahara in many a sheik epic. Access to the beach is gated, but the beach is open daily to 6 p.m.

The road is two-lane. Artichoke fields rim the road. The path winds up onto the dunes, with sand drifting onto the road. The colors are marvelous—the golden sands with hummocks sprouting green grass butch haircuts, the green of the Santa Maria River plain, the blue of the sky and the blue of the ocean and the long, white combers carrying across the almost straight coastline.

The road ends at 15 miles. Return and turn right on Highway 1 (19.6). As usual, Highway 1 is difficult to bicycle. It rarely seems to have a decent shoulder, and the situation continues here. There may be a breeze from the northwest to help along the way in this open area. The road goes up and over the railroad track and follows the base of the Casmalia Hills. To the left is Guadalupe Lake, usually dry and being farmed. The land seems all stripes in browns and greens. Low hills make the way interesting as the road swings slowly toward the southeast past the Rancho Maria Golf Course.

Turn left on Solomon Road (28.8) past cattle, horse and sheep farms, crossing

Orcutt Creek, and into the outskirts of Orcutt. Turn left again on Blosser (29.6) and then right on Foster (30.3).

A ride past the end of the Santa Maria Airport runway and a left on Highway 135 (31.3) will start the bicyclist north toward Waller Park. At Waller Lane turn left into the park. The mileage is 32.9.

32 THROUGH THE CASMALIA HILLS

Distance: *32 miles*
Loop
Traffic: *light to moderate*
Rating: *moderate*

A ride through the Casmalia Hills in the winter and spring is a delight. The new grasses on the hills following the winter rains, and then, in the spring, the wild-flowers, make this one of those scenic wonders of the Central Coast. Casmalia itself isn't much — a town bypassed by growth, resting comfortably in a small valley. Progress is not its aim, if there is an aim. But the ride is pleasant and the smells are full of the good earth and grass. Summer and fall are not to be feared, for the area is cool. The sea breeze wafts the Alaskan Current air on-shore and subdues the effects of the sun.

The ride will get underway from Waller Park in Santa Maria. The park is on Highway 135. Take the Highway 101 off-ramp at Betteravia Road, heading west, and turn left, to the south, on Highway 135, to the park.

From the park pedal south (to the right) on the 135 Expressway and then turn right onto Skyway Drive (0.7). Skyway is a wide, two-lane route with a bike lane that leads by the Santa Maria Airport and the new Santa Maria Industrial Park. Turn left opposite the second Industrial Parkway intersection onto Fairway Avenue (2.5) and bounce along a rural road in the shade of eucalyptus trees. The trees are a few of the 40,000 planted in the late 1800s as windbreaks to keep crops from blowing away. Turn right on A Street (3.1), a nook-and-cranny road. Turn left again on Betteravia Road (3.5), again with a bike lane.

At the Y in the road, bear left (4.1) onto Mahoney Road and then merge onto Black Road (5.4).

Black Road begins the undulations that indicate the flat Santa Maria Valley is being left behind. Cattle graze in one

spot and houses sprout in another. Cross Highway 1 and begin the climb into the Casmalia Hills. Two climbs and two downhills bring one into the Casmalia Valley. The Casmalia Oil Field is one of several in the area that has been pumping oil from the strata for many years.

Casmalia may be visited with a right turn onto the Point Sal Road (10.8). Casmalia comes from the Spanish for *Casa Malo*, a house built by a man named Malo. The area was at one time a Mexican land grant rancho. The road used to go through to Point Sal, but has been blocked off by the Air Force as part of Vandenberg Air Force Base. Both Point Sal and Casmalia Beach were shipping centers in the late 1800s before the railroads came through. Casmalia had a "chute" landing. Goods, including cattle, had to be lowered by cable from the cliffs to the wharf and waiting ships. The only point of interest in Casmalia is the Hitching Post, a popular barbecue steak restaurant that looks like a warehouse. There is a cafe and the General Store, where snacks can be purchased.

Returning to the Lompoc-Casmalia Road, turn right (12.0) and pull up the hill out of the valley and onto Vandenberg Air Force Base property. The hill tops out after a mile and a half, with views ahead of the Santa Ynez Mountains. The huge white golf balls perched on platforms are tracking stations. Vandenberg missiles are fired into polar orbit, for they can be launched south over the ocean without endangering people on land. The first missile was fired in 1958.

The land changes from the rounded grass-topped hills near Casmalia to chaparral-covered hills showing the white limestone bones beneath. The road slips down toward the San Antonio Valley. Y left onto San Antonio Road (16.3) and begin a pleasant pedal through a tiny valley surrounded by low

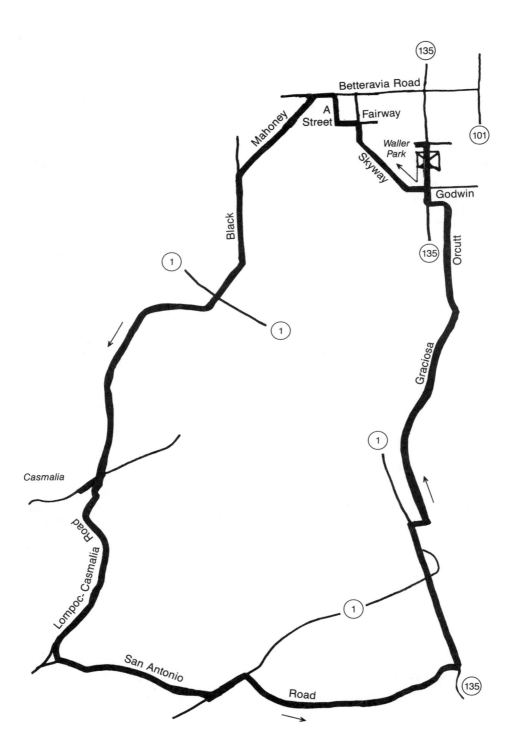

hills. In the far distance are the San Rafael Mountains. Turn left (19.0) on the Vandenberg Road, and then right onto San Antonio East (19.5), dropping again into the San Antonio Valley. The road is as quiet as the countryside — the creak of a windmill, the lowing of cattle, the whirr of the bicycle.

Turn left onto Highway 135 (23.3), a four-lane road, and pedal up the long, easy incline of Harris Canyon. Turn right off the highway (26.1) onto Graciosa. Graciosa parallels the freeway, which will be above. The road is the old highway, with only an occasional motor vehicle. The low rolling hills of the Graciosa Ridge on the right and the Casmalia Hills on the left part for the highway. Derelict barns, brown and white cattle, and old farmhouses lean against the side of the road.

As the road comes into Orcutt, Graciosa crosses Rice Ranch Road and becomes Orcutt Road, paralleling the 135 Expressway. Past Clark Lane there is a bike route, but traffic is moderate through this area, moving in and out of stores and parking lots, and should be watched with eagle eye. At Goodwin Road, Orcutt spills onto the expressway. Continue north on the expressway to the signal at Waller Lane, and turn left to the park (31.7).

33 THROUGH THE SOLOMON HILLS

Distance: *30 miles*
Loop
Traffic: *light to moderate*
Rating: *moderate*

The Solomon Hills are named for the notorious bandito Salomon Pico (Americans do not spell well), who used to hide in these hills while thinking up nefarious plots against the stagecoach trade. He was the man who inspired the tales of Zorro, the dashing hero of book, legend and television. Pico was from an upstanding Northern California family and no one seemed to realize that by day he was a gentleman and by night a highway robber. His gang holed up in the Solomon Hills and robbed travelers on El Camino Real between Los Alamos and the Santa Maria Valley. It is said he buried some of his treasure in the area, but the only treasure to be found has been cattle and oil.

The road will take the bicyclist through some of the lovely back canyons of the area and past the Frémont-Foxen Monument, where Lt. Col. John C. Frémont camped on his way to capture California for the Union.

Los Alamos, just off Highway 101 at Highway 135, will start us on our way. The town boasts motels and restaurants. Take Highway 101 south from Los Alamos aboard the bicycle. It is a four-lane freeway, but there is a wide shoulder and bicycles are permitted. At Alisos Canyon (2.1), turn left into the Solomon Hills along a pleasant two-lane road with little or no traffic. The upward grade is easy through the valley that cuts the comfortably rolling hills. Cattle country stretches away on both sides, the grasslands dotted with cattle and huge oaks. The quiet climb peaks out at 7.9 and begins a drop into Foxen Canyon. This can be hot country, but most of the time it is pleasant, summer and winter. Spring is glorious with the bright green grass and the margins of the road sprinkled with brilliant wildflowers.

Turn left on Foxen Canyon Road (8.5) into an upland valley running through the Solomon Hills. Foxen Canyon is named after Benjamin Foxen, an Englishman who married a Spanish senorita and became a ranchero in the area. The canyon was once on the stagecoach run and Foxen's adobe was one of the stops on the way to Santa Maria.

Asphaltum Creek joins the road as the canyon narrows. Just across a bridge, on the left side of the road (13.0), is a large granite marker called the Frémont-Foxen Monument. The monument marks the area where Frémont camped in December, 1846, on his way south to take Santa Barbara without firing a shot. California was ceded to the United States three weeks later, January 13, 1847. Foxen acted as guide for Frémont, an action that ostracized him in the community. He was forced to seek shelter in Santa Barbara, abandoning his ranch for several years.

The contour of the land begins to change as dark green oaks spill down the canyons into the valley. On a bluff east of the road is the white Sisquoc Church, built as a memorial to Foxen by his children. The road drops into the Sisquoc River Valley. Extensive vineyards are planted in the area as the countryside opens. Other crops include broccoli, cauliflower and sand.

Turn left on Palmer Road (19.5) in Sisquoc and head into hills that are heavily drilled for oil in the Cat Canyon oil fields. At the intersection with Cat Canyon Road, remain on Palmer, to the right. It is possible to take the Cat Canyon Road over Gato Ridge and down Howard Canyon to Highway 101, but there is a miserable uphill grade. Mileage to 101 via Cat Canyon is 9.1. The recommendation is to stay on Palmer, which is a mile shorter and a much easier grade. Through the area the bicyclist can close his or her eyes

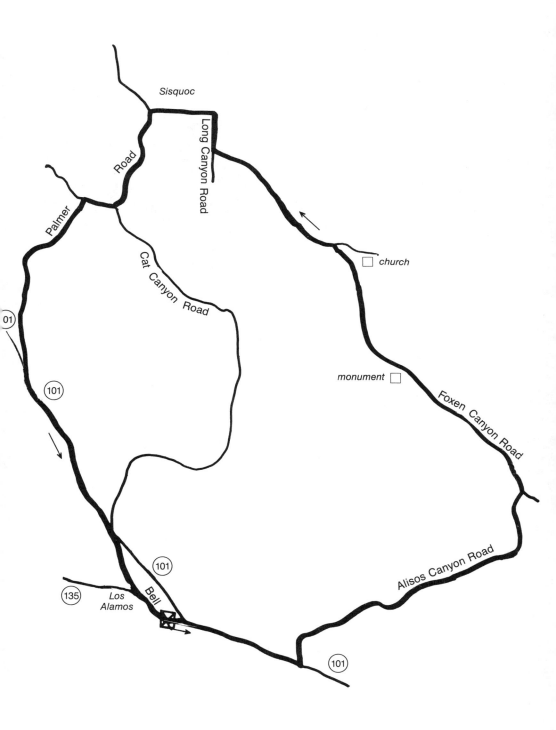

Sisquoc

Long Canyon Road

Road

Palmer

01

101

Cat Canyon Road

church

monument

Foxen Canyon Road

101

135

Bell

Los
Alamos

101

Alisos Canyon Road

101

and still know the road leads through an oil field. The noise and smell will be clues.

Palmer Road continues winding its way up and across a low saddle, topping out about 24 miles through sagebrush and grasslands. A run downhill and a left turn onto Highway 101 (25.7) will take the pedaler off to Los Alamos. Take the Los Alamos exit (28.4) and slip down the old highway. Cross San Antonio Creek, merge onto Highway 135, and pedal into town. Los Alamos was founded in 1876. On the right is the old Union Hotel, built in 1880 and still serving dinners. A little farther along the main street, Bell, is the General Store, another restored Victorian business. It too was built in 1880 and is a State Historical Monument. A return to the starting point puts the mileage at 30.3.

34 LOS ALAMOS AND THE PURISIMA HILLS

Distance: *42 miles*
Loop
Traffic: *light to moderate*
Rating: *difficult*

The little town of Los Alamos, just off Highway 101, is the base for this loop over the Purisima Hills, along the Santa Rita Valley, again through the hills, and back through the beautiful Los Alamos Valley. Los Alamos and Los Alamos Valley are the site of the Mexican land grant given in 1839 to the commandant of the Santa Barbara Presidio. He got first choice of the grants in Santa Barbara County, and he chose this beautiful valley area for his 49,000-acre rancho. The ride should be started early in the day before the westerlies begin blowing around noon in the Santa Rita Valley.

Starting point will be the intersection of Highway 101 and Highway 135 (Bell Street) in Los Alamos. Head west into town on Bell, which is named after the man who purchased 14,000 acres of Los Alamos Rancho and first built a house in the area in the 1870s. Around 1875 the stagecoach was routed through Los Alamos, and a hotel and other accommodations for travelers were built. On Bell Street, on the left, is Los Alamos General Store, built in the 1880s and restored. It is a cornucopia of delight, with food, gifts, handcrafts and other items for sale. At Centennial Street (0.4) turn left. The street was the boundary between Los Alamos and La Laguna land grant ranchos, and was named in honor of America's centennial celebration.

The road slips out of town, past Los Alamos County Park, and almost immediately begins an uphill pull that will take the bicyclist through the Purisima Hills and down Drum Canyon. There

are few cars on the Drum Canyon Road as it climbs up through Canada de las Calaveras. *Calavera* is Spanish for hot-headed fellow. The day I went through, it was hot, and the sun beat down on my head, cooking my brains. Well-named canyon.

The uphill portion is about three miles in length, along a narrow, very winding road that climbs inexorably to a slight crease in the oak-covered hill. Vegetation is dense and here and there shade spills onto the road from the low, deep green trees. The ridge tops out at 3.6 and a lovely downhill ensues. Here the sunny side of the hill changes the vegetation to sage and scrub oaks. The road runs into a long, narrow valley along Santa Rosa Creek past an occasional farmhouse with chickens in the road.

At Highway 246 (9.6) turn right and pedal through the Santa Rita Valley. The area is one you want to avoid in the afternoon, for the winds are right in your teeth and a pleasant ride can become a bear of a ride.

Take the right turn to La Purisima Mission and Vandenberg Air Force Base (16.9). The road is narrow with no shoulder, but traffic is fairly light. La Purisima Mission is at 17.8. It is a state historical park and well worth a visit. The mission building was constructed in 1818 after the devastating earthquake of 1812 destroyed the original building. La Purisima was the 11th in the string of 21 California missions. The pink coloration is authentic, mixed with native materials.

At the signal, continue straight ahead on Highway 1 North (19.8). This is a four-lane road with wide shoulders that climbs up a moderately steep hill past Vandenberg Village, where there are restaurants and grocery stores, should supplies be needed. Past the village on the left is a road to the Federal Correctional Institute, a federal prison that became famous for its Watergate crowd. The road rolls up and down over several ridges and canyons and then flattens near the main gate to Vandenberg Air Force Base. Base housing is on the right, and across the way is the entrance to the base that fires missiles into a north-south trajectory over the Pacific Missile Range.

Turn right at the signal on the Vandenberg Road (26.3) toward Santa Maria. Glimpses of the Pacific can be caught to the left. The large white round objects on the hills are radar tracking stations. Missile launching silos are visible off to the left. The road moves through a canyon and then swings downward. At San Antonio Road East (29.3), turn right and pedal into a quiet little valley hemmed in by low rolling hills. The creak of a windmill may be the only sound. Cattle eye the bicyclist.

At the juncture with Highway 1 take Highway 135 (33.7) toward Los Alamos. With luck the wind will pick up at this point and blow you comfortably through this pastoral valley.

The road swings into Los Alamos. On the right is the Union Hotel, built in 1880 for the stagecoach passengers, later to serve the narrow gauge railroad passengers, and now to serve the motoring public. A return to the starting point finds the mileage at 42.5.

35 THE LOVELY LOS ALAMOS VALLEY

Distance: *32 miles*
Out and back
Traffic: *light*
Rating: *easy*

I could not help but include this lovely little pedal through an east-west valley that catches the light from the sun in morning and afternoon, and that lies hidden from most eyes, a special treat for the slower rhythms of bicycling. The roads are included on three other rides, but not all together, and I would not want someone with a morning or afternoon free, or even a day, to miss this because the other rides are more difficult or fill more of a day, not leaving enough time. This ride is sheer, unadulterated joy. It is not a challenge and it is not macho and it may not even get the aerobic system going. Who cares? It is like riding across the Golden Gate Bridge. Take your time. Enjoy, enjoy.

Los Alamos is in the mild-weather belt, where morning fog burns off early and a warming sun seems to glow day in and day out. Summers may get into the 90s, and winters may drop into the 50s, but mostly the temperature is 65 to 85 degrees year-round. If there is a wind, it blows from the west in the afternoon. Be forewarned. The town itself was founded in 1876, and there are several old buildings of interest. There are motels and restaurants for an overnight stay.

Hop aboard the bicycle and head west on Highway 135, which is the main street. Bell Street was named for the Bell family, early pioneers. Thomas Bell bought 14,000 acres of the Los Alamos land grant, and his son John Stewart Bell became a leading livestock man in the area. The stagecoach to the Santa Maria Valley used to run up this way and Los Alamos was one of the stagecoach stops.

At the Y in the road (0.4), bear left and pedal along the flat valley. The Purisima Hills are to the left, the Solomon Hills to the right. The Solomon Hills are named for Salomon Pico, a famous bandit who became known in fiction as Zorro.

The creek off to the right and then passing under the road to the left is San Antonio Creek. The valley is farmed for grain, and cattle discuss the best blades on the hillsides. Make a left turn to Vandenberg AFB onto San Antonio

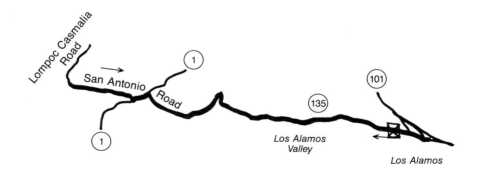

Road (9.0). Dip back into another pleasant valley. San Antonio Creek flows out of the Los Alamos Valley into the San Antonio Valley and thence into the sea.

The road climbs up to Highway 1, the Vandenberg Road. Turn left (13.0) and pedal half a mile to San Antonio West and turn right. Again the pathway is through a quiet valley, although indications that you are on Vandenberg Air Force Base are notable. The large white golf ball on the right horizon is one of many tracking stations on the missile base. To go as far as possible on this pleasant pedal, turn around at the Lompoc-Casmalia Road (16.9). With the wind at your back, you should blow home.

Coming into Los Alamos, note the yellow Victorian, built in 1864, the Union Hotel, built in 1880, and the General Store, also built in 1880.

The end of the ride is 32.2.

36 LA PURISIMA MISSION

Distance: *35 miles*
Loop
Traffic: *light to moderate*
Rating: *moderate to difficult*

One of the most outstanding of California's restored missions is Misíon la Purísima Concepcíon de María Santísima, now La Purisima Mission State Historic Park. The original mission was built in 1787, the 11th in the chain of 21, but was destroyed in an earthquake in 1812 when the roof collapsed, crushing several Indians at Mass. The site was abandoned, and in 1818 a new church was built in La Canada de los Berros, three miles away.

The road to La Purisima winds through typical Central Coast hills and valleys on an old road with few automobiles, and returns on a two-lane highway that renders most hills and dales tame. It is best to leave in the morning before the prevailing westerlies get underway. If the route is well-timed, you will bicycle west with no wind and then blow back. Lompoc is notoriously cool and notoriously windy. Be prepared for a change in temperature.

The starting point will be in Buellton, on Highway 101, at Andersen's Restaurant. There are restaurants, motels and camping facilities in Buellton. Andersen's Restaurant is at the corner of

Highway 246 and Avenue of the Flags. Head south on Avenue of the Flags, out of town and across the Santa Ynez River. Turn right on Santa Rosa Road (0.9). On the left is the Vega Vineyards Winery, where the tasting room is open Fridays and Saturdays. The old barn has been a sight along Highway 101 for many years. It was built in 1853 and is now the tasting room. The adobe house, also built in 1853, can be seen to the right of the barn, hiding under vines as it has for well over one hundred years. The area was once Rancho La Vega (the meadow), part of Rancho Santa Rosa, Mexican land grant of 1845.

Santa Rosa Road continues along the bluffs above the Santa Ynez River through farm and ranch country. The wide road narrows after six miles and the country grows more hilly, as does the road.

Santa Rosa Park is at 8.3. There are restroom and picnic facilities down the half-mile-long road into the park, which clings to the side of the mountain with some tenacity. Past the park and over a ridge the road swings down into a side valley, which in spring is often planted to flowers, used for seed. The smells are enough to knock one off the bicycle. The road climbs back through a pinch in the valley called the Lompoc Narrows. After crossing another side valley the road

climbs to Highway 1 (16.9). Turn right and speed into the outskirts of Lompoc.

Turn right at the intersection of Highway 246 (18.4). There is a small park for overnight camping and day use, River Park (18.8). A Y left onto Purisima Road (20.2) leads to La Purisima Mission State Historic Park (20.6). The red tile roof of the mission, nestled in the small canyon, marks the way. The park is open 7 a.m. to 7 p.m. daily.

The rangers suggest a two-hour stroll through the extensive grounds, mission, padres' residence, garden and lavenderia. Stop at the museum to get a tour guide and pay the nominal fee. Among the highlights is the sense of peace that the mission has. It is rarely crowded and people stroll leisurely about the grounds and buildings. The tracks of El Camino Real meander through the grounds near the mission. There is a pen for animals, an Indian cemetery, the long narrow church with its altar, the soldiers' quarters, the buttressed residence building, the padres' private chapel, the water system, and the mission garden where grow many native plants used by the missionaries and the Indians.

Leaving the mission, turn left on the Lompoc-Vandenberg Road and left again (21.6) onto Highway 246. If the wind has come up and it is strong enough, there will be hardly any pedaling to return to Buellton. Youngsters from Buellton used to bicycle west on the Lompoc-Buellton Road in the morning and then set homemade sails to sail-cycle home.

It is a straight shot into Buellton through farm land. There has been a settlement in Buellton, connected with Buell Ranch, since 1883. The ranch was part of the 26,643-acre Mexican land grant Rancho San Carlos de Jonata, granted in 1846. The present-day elementary school in Buellton is named Jonata.

The intersection of Highway 246 and Avenue of the Flags marks the end of the ride (34.5).

37 BALLARD, FOXEN CANYONS FIGURE EIGHT

Distance: *23 miles*
Loop
Traffic: *light to moderate*
Rating: *moderate*

This figure-eight loop will take the
bicyclist through some of the nicest
country in the Central Coast — pleasant, winding roads, rolling hills studded
with coastal oaks, an occasional winery,
cattle grazing in the liquid light. And it
will close at one of California's famed
Franciscan missions.

The journey starts in the Danish community of Solvang, reached by driving
three miles east of Buellton on Highway
246 where it intersects with Highway
101. The Solvang Park will be the starting point, located on Mission Drive
(Highway 246) between the two signals.

Head west on Mission and turn right
at the signal, which is Atterdag Road.
In the second block is the Solvang
Elementary School, with a Danish stork
for good luck atop its red tile roof. Just
north is Bethania Lutheran Church in
typical Danish Gruntvig architectural
style. It was built in 1927. On the right
atop the hill is the Solvang Lutheran
Home. At one time Atterdag College
stood on this knoll. A Danish folk college, it was the original focus of the
town, but it closed in 1937 and was torn
down in 1970.

The road speeds out of town past
Hans Christian Andersen Park and a
residential area and into the countryside. The name of the road is now Chalk
Hill. At the intersection with Ballard
Canyon Road (1.5) go straight ahead,
north. The road begins a slow climb
toward the Los Olivos ridge. As the
valley narrows, so does the road. At the
head a sudden upswing of a third of a
mile crests with views of the San Rafael
Mountains. At your feet is the little town
of Los Olivos.

A short sweep down the hill and
across Highway 154 (7.0) will put the
bicyclist on Foxen Canyon Road. Con-

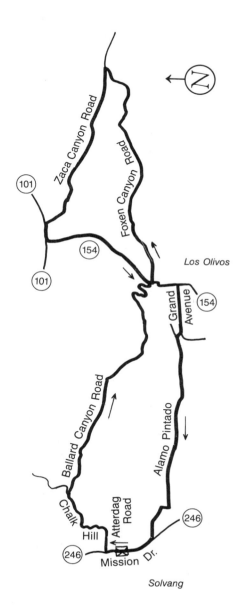

tinue north through another flat valley rimmed with low hills. A short one-third-mile uphill will put you on the top of a ridge, looking down to the left on the rust-brown roof of Firestone Winery. From the ridge top the road does a pleasant plunge into Zaca Canyon, across Zaca Creek, and a sudden left turn (11.0) onto Zaca Station Road will send the bicyclist southwest toward the Firestone Vineyards. The wine tasting room is open 10 a.m. to 4 p.m. daily.

The road continues down through the flat valley to busy Highway 101 (14.2). Make a left turn across the four lanes and prepare to make another left turn in three-tenths of a mile onto Highway 154, the San Marcos Pass Road.

Highway 154 supports moderate traffic, but there is a wide shoulder. Pump back into the hills. The countryside continues to be a handsome mixture of grassland and oaks. The hills top out at 16 miles and then send one on a speedy downhill to Los Olivos. Jig in on the right to Mattei's Tavern (17.0), the white frame building almost hidden under vines. The tavern was built in 1886 to serve patrons of the narrow gauge railroad that chugged to town from the north. A stagecoach picked the passengers up and transported them over San Marcos Pass to Santa Barbara.

The road you are on is Railroad Avenue. Continue east to Grand Avenue, turn right (17.3), and pedal through Los Olivos. The tiny town was founded in 1887 to serve the railroad and stage-coach passengers. It is in a revival at the moment, with new western-style shops and stores.

Continue south to the Y in the road (18.1) and bear right across a bridge over Alamo Pintado Creek and then left onto Alamo Pintado Road. The valley is farmed and ranched in small acreages and everything from olives to walnuts to sheep to cattle to hay is grown. Turn right at Highway 246, Mission Drive (22.3), and pump up the hill into Solvang.

A treat at this point is a visit to Old Mission Santa Inés. Founded in 1804,

it is the 19th in the chain of 21 California missions. It fell into disrepair and ruins, but restoration on a small scale began in 1904 and with additional funds on a large scale in 1947. There are tours and a gift shop and museum that are open during the summer from 9 a.m. to 5 p.m. and during the winter from 9:30 a.m. to 4:30 p.m. On Sundays the hours are noon to 4:30 p.m.

Continue on into Solvang to the park (23.1).

38 FIGUEROA MOUNTAIN

Distance: *39 miles*
Loop
Traffic: *light*
Rating: *very difficult*

Figueroa Mountain is a journey up the side of a mountain, across a ridge to a second mountain and down a steep road to the valley below. Views into the San Rafael Wilderness area, the Santa Ynez Valley, and down into Lake Cachuma reward the ardent bicyclist. Midsummer can be hot, in the 90s, but there is usually a cooling breeze in the afternoon. Spring is a lovely time, for the area is rich in wildflowers. On weekends the traffic during spring may push up toward the moderate mark, but usually there is not much doing in these hills. During the winter months, check with the Solvang Sheriff's Substation as to

whether the road is open. Figueroa Mountain is the kingpin because it is the most defined. The elevation is 4,528. Ranger Peak is higher, about 4,680, but not as noticeable from the valley below.

The trip will start in Los Olivos, about three miles east of Highway 101, on the San Marcos Pass Road, Highway 154.

Figueroa Mountain Road, a north extension of Grand Avenue, heads north from Highway 154 in Los Olivos, up Alamo Pintado Canyon. Large farms and ranches grow alfalfa hay, cattle and horses. About four miles up the valley is Midland School, a private residential school in a semi-primitive setting.

At about six miles the road crosses the creek at Birbent Canyon on a narrow one-lane bridge, elevation about 1,300 feet, and begins its climb toward

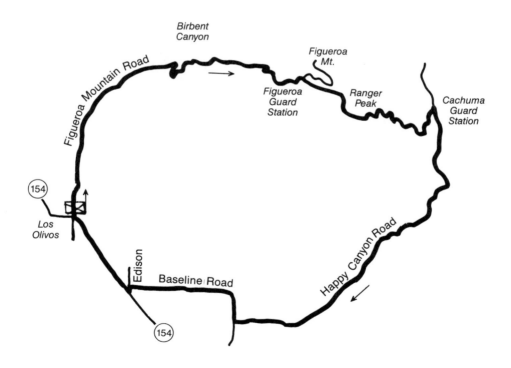

Figueroa. This south (and hot) slope catches the daylong sun, and brush and scrub oak are sparse. Digger pines and sage dot the hillsides. A vein of serpentine is exposed at various road cuts. At about 10 miles the road crosses into Los Padres National Forest with the elevation about 2,400. Figueroa Station is at 11.6 miles with lots of uphill yet to go. Elevation is 3,000 feet. At 12 miles stands of pines and firs indicate the elevation is about 3,600. The dirt road to Figueroa Mountain lookout and the top of the peak itself is at 12.2. The road will climb from 3,600 to 4,500 in a mile and a half. However, the paved road leads us on to Figueroa Camp (13.1). There are picnic and restroom facilities, and camping is available.

Most of the uphill work is behind now. Not all, but most. The road continues through the forested ridge on a generally flat course, swinging out of the trees, into scrub and then working back up into the trees again near Ranger Peak. As the road continues there will be views north into the San Rafael Wilderness area. The odd banded rock formation is Hurricane Deck.

The road narrows. Care should be exercised on the downhill sections. The downhill begins at 16 miles. The mountains are precipitous, and old abandoned mines dot the hills. At one vista point, sprawling Cachuma Lake spreads blue fingers into the canyons.

At Cachuma Saddle Guard Station (19.3), turn right and continue the downward path past the old Redrock Mine, where quicksilver was pulled from the rock. There is a short section of road below Cachuma Saddle that is unpaved and "unpassable in wet weather" (says the sign).

As the road swings through Happy Canyon into a more wooded area, you will have to ford Cachuma Creek twice, so beware of traveling too fast and suddenly finding yourself up to your ankles in water. At Cachuma Camp (21.5) there is overnight camping and picnicking. The area is pretty in spring and fall.

Suddenly there are fancy ranches and flatter country. The road improves. There are also cattle crossings and open range, so take care.

The road swings by a large horse breeding and training facility on the right, and comes to an end at Baseline (31.6). Turn right and pedal through a rancho estate area. There may be a wind out of the west, which is the direction you are heading, unfortunately.

Turn left at Edison Street (35.6) and then right on Highway 154 (35.7) to proceed toward Los Olivos. A sweep to the left and into Los Olivos brings the rider back to the starting point (38.7).

39 FOUR TOWNS IN SANTA YNEZ VALLEY

Distance: *16 miles*
Loop
Traffic: *moderate*
Rating: *easy to moderate*

Four of the five towns that comprise the historic and scenic Santa Ynez Valley will be visited on this loop trip. Solvang, the Danish community; Ballard, the tiny home of the little red schoolhouse; Los Olivos, the railroad town that never was; and Santa Ynez, a town retaining its western flavor, all have their special flavors and delights. The countryside between is interesting and sometimes beautiful.

The journey will start in Solvang at the Solvang Park. Solvang may be reached from Highway 101, east of Buellton. It was founded in 1911 by a group of Danes who wanted to build a Danish colony on the West Coast. The focus of the colony would be a folk college, named Atterdag. It stood on a hill just north of town until 1970, a great, white frame structure. It was torn down as a fire hazard. Solvang now, of course, is a tourist mecca, and the streets are jammed on weekends with people enjoying the unique Danish architecture, bakeries, gift stores, and, in evenings during the summer, the Solvang Theaterfest, a repertory theater run by the Pacific Conservatory of the Performing Arts.

Leaving the Solvang Park on Mission Drive, the bicyclist heads east past Old Mission Santa Inés. At the bottom of the hill past the mission, turn left onto Alamo Pintado Road (0.7). The road slips by a shopping center, and continues through the Alamo Pintado Valley toward Ballard. J. Carey Cellars is on the left, where wine may be tasted and tours taken from 10 a.m. to 4 p.m., Tuesday through Sunday. Just beyond the winery, turn right on Baseline Avenue (3.4) and into Ballard.

Ballard was an old stagecoach station,

established in 1860. The town itself was founded in 1881, named for William Ballard, a friend of the founder, George Lewis. What is of interest is the old Ballard store, now a gourmet restaurant, the schoolhouse, and the church. As you pedal by the store, turn left on Cottonwood Street (*Alamo Pintado* means painted cottonwood in Spanish). At the end of the street is the little red schoolhouse, which has been in continuous use since 1883. Go past the schoolhouse and turn right on Lewis Street, returning to Baseline Avenue (4.0) and turn right again. On the right is the old Ballard Presbyterian Church, built in 1898 to serve a congregation that had been meeting in a saloon and then in the schoolhouse. It is now a private funeral chapel, and the new church, Santa Ynez Valley Presbyterian,

has been built across Alamo Pintado Road from Baseline.

Continue west and back to Alamo Pintado Road, turning right and heading north toward Los Olivos. At the Y in the road (5.3), bear right to Grand Avenue and then turn left, heading due north. Los Olivos was founded in 1887 as the southern hub of the narrow gauge Pacific Coast Railroad. Dreams of grandeur faded, however, when Southern Pacific went by the coastal route, through Lompoc. The town is newly sprung to life with fancy Victorian homes, The Grand Hotel and several art galleries. As you come to the flagpole in the middle of town, turn left on Alamo Pintado Street (6.1). Turn right on Nojoqui Avenue to Railway Avenue. On the left is Mattei's Tavern, built in 1886

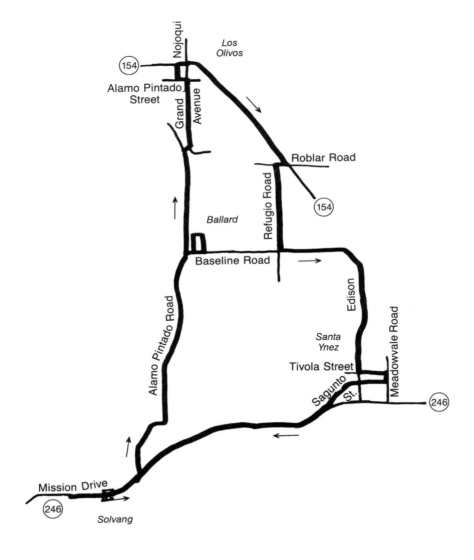

to serve passengers of the narrow gauge railroad, and now restored as a restaurant.

Turn right on Railway to Grand and jig left and right onto Highway 154 (6.5). As the road swings off toward Santa Ynez, the countryside opens and large ranches and homes may be glimpsed in the hills to the east.

At the Roblar Avenue sign, turn right (8.3), and then left on Refugio Road. There are many Arabian horse breeders in the valley and several ranches along this road are members of the Arabian association. Turn left on Baseline Avenue (9.4) and pedal up onto an open plateau. After a turn to the right you will be on Edison Street and coming into Santa Ynez. At Tivola Street, turn left (11.7) and right on Meadowvale Road and right again on Sagunto.

Santa Ynez was founded in 1882. A large, posh hotel was built, as with Los Olivos, to cater the passengers of a train that never came. It burned in 1935. Sagunto is the main street. At the corner of Faraday and Sagunto, on the left, is the Santa Ynez Valley Historical Society Museum, worth a visit should you be pedaling by during its open hours, 1 to 4 p.m., Friday through Sunday. Next to it is the Santa Ynez Branch Library, the first branch library established in California, built in 1912.

Follow Sagunto Street on past the Santa Ynez Park, where picnic facilities are available, and turn right on Highway 246 (12.7). A short pull up the hill and on the right is Santa Ynez Valley High School. A bike path starts at the west end of the campus and will take you for a pleasant ride paralleling the highway, and down into a small arroyo. The path is poorly maintained, but the road has glass. Take your pick.

The path ends at Alamo Pintado Road and the bicyclist is back on the highway and into Solvang. On the left is the Mission Santa Inés, founded in 1804, 19th of the 21 California missions. There are tours, a gift shop and museum open during the summer from 9 a.m. to 5 p.m. and during the winter from 9:30 a.m. to 4:30 p.m. On Sundays the hours are noon to 4:30 p.m.

Continue west on Highway 246 (Mission Drive) to Solvang Park and the end of the circuit (15.9).

40 LAKE CACHUMA

Distance: *25 miles*
Semi-loop
Traffic: *light to moderate*
Rating: *moderate*

Cachuma Lake was to answer all the water problems of Santa Barbara County. But more people flocked to the area and so it does not. But it helps, and it adds a gem of blue to the chaparral hills. The Cachuma project, which became Bradbury Dam, was begun in 1950 and completed in 1953. The seven-mile-long lake, tucked between the Santa Ynez Mountains and the San Rafaels, is a popular fishing and boating area with

a pleasant park and marina. There is overnight camping.

We will start in Solvang, at the Solvang Park, as we have done with many of the rides in this area. Solvang is located three miles east of Highway 101 on Highway 246. The highway becomes Mission Drive in Solvang, and the park is located on Mission at First Street.

Proceed east out of Solvang, past Old Mission Santa Inés, founded in 1804. The road goes down the hill out of town. Just across the bridge, on the left, is the beginning of a bike route that parallels the highway but is down in an arroyo by

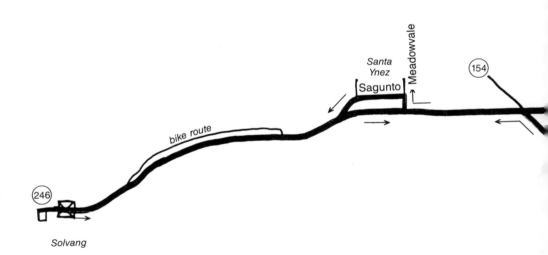

a tiny stream and bordered by oaks. The bike route surfaces at Santa Ynez Valley High School and you will have to cross back again to the right-hand side of Highway 246. The road passes the little town of Santa Ynez, founded in 1882 and retaining its western flavor.

At the juncture with Highway 154, cross onto Armour Ranch Road (5.6), a shoulderless farm road. The road goes up and down through ranching country. Cattle graze the hills and hay is grown in the quiet dales. The road swings around and comes out onto Highway 154 (8.1). Turn left onto the highway, which is a wide two-lane road with a good marked shoulder.

The road crosses the Santa Ynez River, now tamed behind Bradbury Dam and usually dry summer and fall. The area grows more wooded and the road begins to climb into the hills. Up and down it goes, with each valley containing green alfalfa fields.

The road pulls steadily upward to the Bradbury Dam Observation Point (11.4).

Bicycle out to the point, which is just one third of a mile. The 204,000-acre-foot reservoir spreads at one's feet. The earth-filled dam is 275 feet high and 3,000 feet long. The lake took five years to fill.

Return to the highway, which is the San Marcos Pass Road, and turn left. Now the shoulder disappears and the road narrows. Up a hill and down by an inlet, it then comes to the entrance to the park (13.1).

There is a fee to enter, but a nice park, a store, snack bar and marina await. There is a mile or so of roads in the park through the various campgrounds and picnic areas, which are fun to explore. The highway does continue beside the lake for another four miles or so beyond the entrance before it pulls away and up San Marcos Pass.

Back on Highway 154, turn right, west, on the roller coaster ride that leads to the Santa Ynez River (17.3). Continue straight ahead on Highway 154 up the hill as the road goes to a wide two-lane

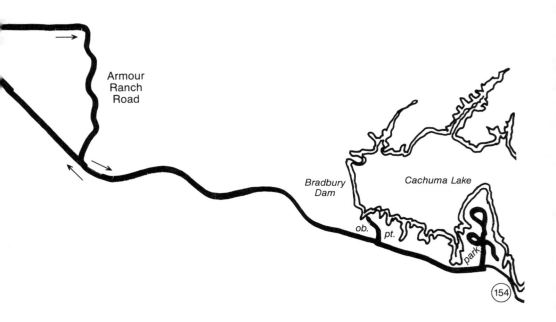

Armour Ranch Road

Bradbury Dam

Cachuma Lake

ob. pt.

park

154

with a wide shoulder. Turn left at the intersection with Highway 246, toward Santa Ynez, Solvang and Buellton (19.3).

As you come to Santa Ynez, turn right on Meadowvale (20.5) and left onto Sagunto Street. The Santa Ynez Valley Historical Society Museum is on the left on the corner of Sagunto and Faraday. It features artifacts from Indian times to Valley pioneers, and includes the Parks-Janeway Carriage House. It is open Fridays through Sundays, 1 to 4 p.m.

Continue on Sagunto until it merges with Highway 246 (21.4). The bike path starts just past the buildings at Santa Ynez Valley High School (22.4) and comes out at Alamo Pintado Creek. Up the road into Solvang and to the park will close out the tour (24.9).

41 JALAMA BEACH

Distance: *38 miles*
Out and back
Traffic: *light*
Rating: *difficult*

Jalama Beach is a wind-swept, isolated beach known for its mammoth waves. If you would like to see Central Coast surfing at its best, Jalama is the place to go. Unobstructed waves beat in against this shore. Surf conditions make for great viewing.

The ride will start in Lompoc, a city of about 33,000, located 20 miles west of Highway 101 on Highway 246. There are at least three good rides out of Lompoc — the Drum Canyon ride, La Purisima Mission ride and Jalama Beach. In the case of Drum Canyon and La Purisima Mission, I started the rides in Los Alamos and Buellton because of the wind, which is going to come up in the Lompoc Valley, blowing from the west, 99 percent of the afternoons. Nonetheless, the rides could have originated in Lompoc. With the Jalama Beach ride the winds are somewhat allayed by the terrain, and the afternoon should see the riders going in the "right" direction.

River Park will be the beginning of our journey. It is located just east of Highway 1 on Highway 246, and has camping, restroom and parking facilities. There are many motels and restaurants in town.

From the park, head south on

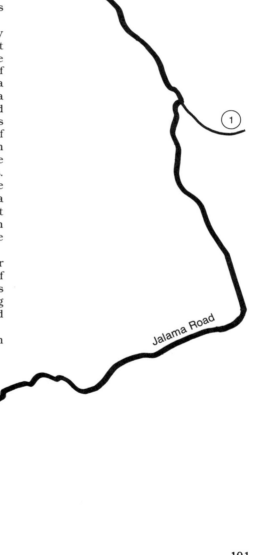

Highway 246 toward Lompoc, and turn left onto Highway 1 (0.4), skirting the city limits. The two-lane, shouldered road leads up through a narrow canyon and out onto an upland of sage and scrub oaks. On the right are tailings from the Johns Manville diatomaceous earth mines. The diatomaceous earth comes from billions of diatoms, a marine algae, when the area was under the sea. Diatomaceous earth is used as an abrasive and in filters.

The road drops into a pleasant valley carved by Salsipuedes Creek. At the intersection with Jalama Road, turn right (4.6). The road climbs away from the valley, following the creek. The farms and ranches through the area are

prosperous. Note the huge red barn on the left about a mile and a half from the turn-off. It must be one of the handsomest barns in the country. Cattle and horses graze on the rolling, oak-dotted hills. About five miles down the road there will be a steep climb of about a mile and a half with wonderful views back toward ridges and ranges of hills. A three-mile downhill rewards the bicyclist as the canyon narrows and beautiful stands of dark green oaks grow over the road. This is classic coastal-range country with impressive ranch and farm lands.

Another climb upward and a glimpse of the Pacific can be caught as the road begins a plunge downward along Jalama Creek. Occasionally, tantalizing views of the ocean burn blue between the gray greens. The road jigs to the left, crosses the railroad tracks and begins a drop to the park. Surfers probably will be glimpsed in the waves just below the road. The road slips into the park (19.0), where there is a concession stand with snack bar.

There are camping, picnicking and restroom facilities. A walk along the shore is imperative, for the breakers are often a sight to behold, and should there be surfers, they are always worth a gasp and a chuckle. The park area near Jalama Creek was once a Chumash Indian village. The park is now 28 acres with 1,600 feet of ocean frontage.

The return will duplicate the ride, with a stiff pull out of Jalama to Highway 1. Turn left at the highway (33.4) and return to Lompoc. Turn right at Highway 246 (37.6) and left at the park (38.0).

42 LAS CRUCES—LOST UNDER ASPHALT

Distance: *43 miles*
Loop
Traffic: *light to moderate*
Rating: *moderate to difficult*
Side trip: *30 miles, difficult*
    (see Jalama Beach)

Las Cruces is a town that has disappeared under a freeway interchange, and the Las Cruces adobe has disappeared behind a fence and under a shelter. But the road there and back is interesting and 75 percent of the time downright beautiful, so why not take a ride to a town that does not exist anymore?

The ride starts in Buellton and there is a choice of roads, one more rural and difficult than the other, but both exactly the same in mileage. The more rural and the more difficult is Santa Rosa Road, which follows the Santa Ynez River for much of its course. Details of that road are in the ride to La Purisima

Mission. For the sake of variety, the easier and more urbanized road, Highway 246, will be described. Where the two meet on Highway 1, the mileage will be the same. The ride should be started in the morning to avoid the afternoon westerlies.

The starting point will be at Highway 246 and Avenue of the Flags, just west of Highway 101, in Buellton. Buellton is the site of the land grant Rancho San Carlos de Jonata. There are motels, restaurants and camping facilities, and the town is a good base for several rides in the area, including those originating in both Solvang and Los Alamos.

Pedal west on Highway 246. It is a broad four-lane road that narrows to a two-lane highway out of town. The road follows the bluffs above the wandering Santa Ynez River, then Y's away and over some low saddles into the Santa Rita Valley. A long downhill, a long uphill and then down past the radio

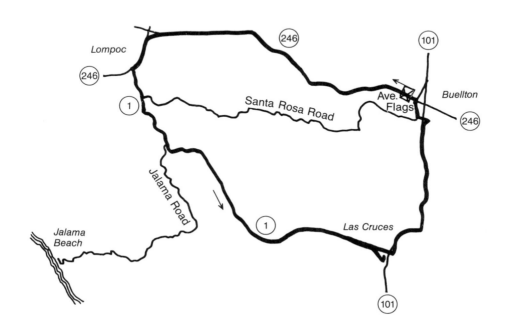

tower, and views of Lompoc open ahead. At the juncture with Highway 1, turn left (16.1). Just before the turn is River Park, where there are restroom and picnic facilities.

Highway 1 climbs up a narrow canyon for a mile and a half. Coming in from the east is Santa Rosa Road. The mileage is 17.6 and bicyclists riding Santa Rosa Road should turn left onto Highway 1. The hills, covered with sage and scrub oak, show the tailings from diatomaceous earth mining. Diatomaceous earth is a fine siliceous earth composed chiefly of the cell walls of diatoms, which are marine algae. The substance is used in filtration and as an abrasive.

The road swoops and curves along the side of Salsipuedes Creek, moving generally upward. The road to Jalama Beach is a 30-mile side trip described in #41 and will increase the mileage on this trip to 73 miles. Good riders might include it as a side trip, or those interested in camping overnight would find it a good half-way camping spot. It is 35 miles from Buellton to Jalama via Lompoc, and 37 miles from Jalama via Las Cruces to Buellton.

Highway 1 gradually climbs up this quiet, rolling countryside. The road crosses back and forth over Ytias and El Jaro creeks, the latter five times. The road tops out at about 30 miles and a delicious downhill of two miles brings the bicyclist to Las Cruces. At 33.0, turn right.

This is the old road and enters Gaviota State Park/Las Cruces Adobe section. As the road slips through the brush, off on the left is a weedy, overgrown dirt road with a wooden one-lane bridge. All are almost lost in the undergrowth. Leave the bicycle and step over the pipe fence barring the way to the adobe, under a shelter and surrounded by a high fence. At one time there were plans to restore the crumbling building, but no progress had been made by 1990, and the adobe seems beyond restoration.

Las Cruces itself was bulldozed under when the highway was made into a freeway intersection. Never much of a town, Las Cruces got its name, "The Crosses," when Franciscan fathers discovered Indian grave mounds, each marked with a wooden cross. There are hot springs south of Las Cruces and at one time, in the 1860s, it became something of a watering hole, with a stagecoach stop, hotel, store, saloon, restaurant, brothel and post office. When Highway 101 was constructed through the area in 1917, the little town began to serve the motoring public, but it never grew and the Las Cruces store closed its doors for the last time in 1957. Hardly anyone noticed its passing when the cloverleaf went right over the top in 1967.

The old Highway 101 bridge still stands, down the road past the adobe, dwarfed under the eight lanes above.

Back on Highway 1, turn right to cross over Highway 101. To the right at the "T" intersection is an additional section of Gaviota State Park. A road that quickly becomes little more than a trail leads from a parking lot to the hot springs. It is about three-quarters of a mile hike into the area.

A left turn will put you on Highway 101 heading north (34.9). This is the five-lane highway north to Buellton with moderate traffic and wide shoulders. The road climbs two miles over Nojoqui Pass and then there is a long downhill along Nojoqui Creek through the middle of the Santa Ynez Mountains. As the road breaks out of the mountains, take the offp-ramp to the right to Santa Rosa Road and Buellton (42.5). Cross over the freeway, turn right onto Avenue of the Flags (42.6) and proceed into Buellton to Highway 246 (43.4).

43 NOJOQUI FALLS

Distance: *17 miles*
Loop
Traffic: *light to moderate*
Rating: *moderate*

In the hills south of Solvang is a lovely little park called Nojoqui, complete with waterfall, limestone cliffs, magnificent oaks, and an old Indian legend. The road to the park is one of the prettiest

in the state, following a meandering stream through a thicket of oaks and cottonwoods and sycamores and ferns and poison oak (watch where you stop to rest). Once on the high plateau there is the park, nestled in the Santa Ynez Mountains, then a brisk run down Highway 101 to Buellton, and a return to the home of Danish pastries.

The route starts at the Solvang Park

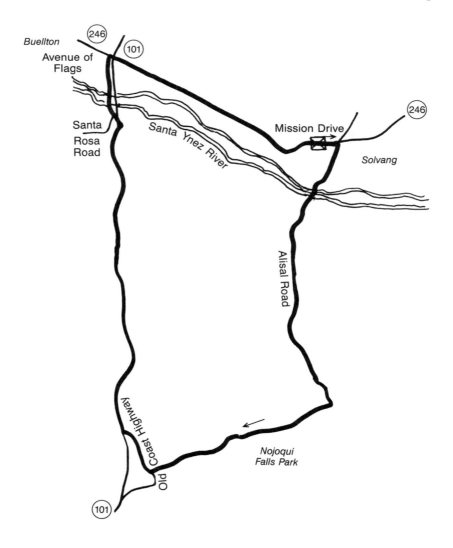

on Mission Drive (Highway 246, three miles east of Highway 101) between First and Second streets. Head east on Mission for one block to the signal at Alisal Road and turn right. You will be in the middle of the Danish provincial architecture for which Solvang is so famous. On the left just before leaving the business district of town is the only Danish-styled United States Post Office building. And of course there is one Danish windmill to zip by. There are more windmills per capita in Solvang than in Denmark itself.

The road plunges out of town and down to the Santa Ynez River, dry much of the year after the building of the dam at Cachuma Lake. Across the river is the Alisal Ranch, which combines a residential area above a golf course; a resort with tennis courts and swimming pool and rodeo grounds; plus a working cattle ranch. The grounds are beautiful and the road is quiet. It slowly moves upward and becomes narrow and windy, shaded and cool. Very gradually it steepens. Bright sunlight filters through the green shade. After a mile of uphill, the road breaks through the end of the Alisal Canyon and comes out into the sun, through a rolling upland. On the left is the crest of the Santa Ynez Mountains, darkly shaded in deep green. A tiny creek called Monjas babbles along the side of the road during a wet year.

The park is on the left at 6.4 miles. Turn in and bicycle to the end of the road. There are picnic facilities and restrooms in the park, but the attraction is the waterfall, which is a quarter-mile walk in from road's end.

The word Nojoqui is Chumash and may have meant, in that lost language, "honeymoon." There are several legends, including a tragic love story, but there is one myth that explains how the falls came to be. The story goes that there was a great drought, and the chief of the Chumash prayed to the Great Spirit for water. The Spirit led the chief over the dry land up a canyon, where he

prayed all night. In the morning, an Indian maiden in a long white gown appeared in the canyon and took the chief to a fern-covered dell. "This is for you and your people," said the maiden, and rose toward the Morning Star, trailing her gown across the ferns and rocks. The gown turned to a ribbon of water. And that is what you will see at the falls, a gossamer gown of satin ribbons cascading down the limestone cliffs.

Back at Alisal Road (6.9), a turn to the left will send you past an open area of the park that was once a stagecoach stop and post office serving travelers along the old Gaviota road between Gaviota and Santa Inés Mission and also between Gaviota and Mattei's Tavern in Los Olivos. The road slants down toward Nojoqui Pass's north side. At the boulevard stop on Old Coast Highway (7.7) turn right. Busy Highway 101 looms ahead, but for one mile you will be traveling on the old highway, made of cement, that served for many years, winding down along the side of Nojoqui Creek. At the highway (8.7), turn right on the wide shoulder and speed down the easy grade to Buellton. Use caution on the bridges, which have no shoulder for slow-moving bicyclists.

The four-lane road zips through cattle country and across the Santa Ynez River into the Santa Ynez Valley. Take the Buellton off-ramp at Santa Rosa Road (12.8), turn left to cross over the freeway, right on Avenue of the Flags and proceed into Buellton, the home of Split-Pea Soup. Andersen's famous restaurant is at the corner of the Avenue of Flags and Highway 246. Turn right (13.6) on Highway 246, cross back over Highway 101 and proceed along the Buellton-Solvang Road. This is a wide two-lane road with a somewhat narrow shoulder. The traffic is moderate and moving fast. On either side of the road are several horse breeding farms.

Past an ersatz castle and up the hill into Solvang, past motel row and the shops (if you can get past the shops) and back to the park. Mileage is 17.3.

44 THE PRESIDENT'S HIGHWAY

Distance: *39 miles*
Loop
Traffic: *light to moderate*
Rating: *very difficult*
Moderate variation: *out and back,*
14 miles

The President's Highway refers to Refugio Road, part dirt, that goes by Rancho del Cielo, the Western White House (1981–1989), high atop the Santa Ynez Mountains. All you will see of the former Western White House is a locked gate on a private road, but the ride itself is splendid if you don't mind seven miles of uphill, three on a dirt and bedrock road. El Camino Real used to come this way, when it was a horse and cart road, from Santa Barbara over Refugio Pass and into the Santa Ynez Valley and to the Santa Inés Mission, then on to La Purisima Mission at Lompoc.

This route could be started at Refugio State Beach where there are camping facilities, but I am taking the starting point in Solvang, which has excellent facilities. I prefer the clockwise circuit, mostly because I prefer going uphill on a dirt road rather than downhill on a dirt road. There are those who may differ. I have a tendency to walk my bicycle on dirt if the surface is bad (and it is bad), and I would rather walk uphill than walk downhill, which must be considered a terrible waste. Refugio Road may be impassable following a heavy rain.

Solvang is located three miles east of Highway 101 at Buellton. From the Solvang Park on Mission Drive (Highway 246), head east. Down the hill out of town and across the bridge is a bike route on the left side of the road. There is a wide shoulder here on the two-lane highway, but the bike route is an interesting, if bumpy, variation. It rejoins the highway at Santa Ynez Valley High School. Just past the high school, turn right onto Refugio Road (2.7) and pedal across the valley, past several horse ranches. Among the breeds in the

area are Traekner, Thoroughbred and Arabian.

Beyond the bridge at Mahoney Crossing (4.2), the road narrows and winds up toward Refugio Pass, following the contour of the land, and it is a bumpy land. Sycamores and oaks overhang the road as it moves through a pleasant area next to Quiota Creek. The creek passes back and forth under and over the road, depending on whether the year is wet or dry. You are more likely to see cowboys than bicycle riders in this area, although this is a favorite ride to the end of the paved road for local bicyclists.

The canyon is particularly beautiful in spring and fall — spring for its green grass and bright wildflowers, and fall for its yellow and red leaves. The pavement ends at 6.9 miles and short ride bicyclists will want to turn back for an out-and-back ride of 14 miles. Those who plan to forge ahead, however, will find a very rough road that has eroded to bedrock in several areas. You will have to walk road bikes on some steep pitches. On the flatter areas, some oiled, there is reasonable pedaling.

The steepness grows apace and at times the road is no more than one lane wide. Views north of the Santa Ynez Valley and the San Rafael Mountains begin to open. The dampness of the canyon, particularly in the spring, brings out the smells of the good earth, of blossoms, of leaves in an intoxicating mixture as heady as a cold watermelon on a hot day. The road widens and then tops out at 10.2 when the pavement begins (thank heaven) at the juncture with Camino Cielo. The elevation is 2,250, an elevation gain of about 1,800 feet in seven miles; about 1,300 feet in the last three miles.

The road winds along the crest for a time and then begins its descent. At 10.7 a road to the right with a locked gate, 3333 Refugio Pass Road, is the road to Rancho del Cielo (Ranch of the Sky) and to Rancho Dos Vistas. The gate has always been locked, even before

President Reagan's advent. On old topo maps the ranch is called Tip Top. There are several ranches along the crest of the mountains. The President's consisted of about 688 acres, most in brush and oaks, and ran about 30 head of cattle. The ranch was homesteaded by José Jesús Pico in 1880. He built the adobe, which was the house used by President Reagan and Mrs. Reagan, around 1898. There were several homesteaders in the area and a one-room schoolhouse was built on the Pico Ranch to educate the youngsters of the settlement. The ranch was sold in 1944 for $6,000 and was appraised in 1980 at $2 million. President Reagan bought the ranch in 1974.

There may be a few people around, but mostly the sound is of a distant hawk, a whisper of wind and the click of a bicycle. As the road plunges downward the flora changes from a wet north slope to a dry south slope of chaparral and madrone. Views of the Santa Barbara Channel and the Pacific Ocean open out as the mountains dive to the sea.

Stop occasionally on the way to cool the brakes and enjoy the view. One switchback will allow views to the east of Goleta. Watch out for cattle guards, chuckholes and, near the bottom, a

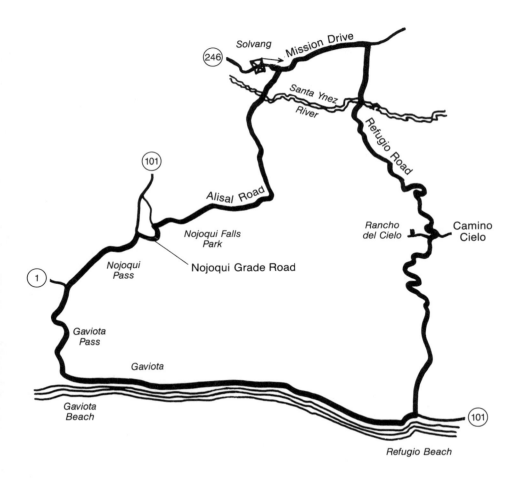

bridge is Refugio State Beach, which has facilities. Turn right for 101 North (17.1). Traffic is moderate and moving, but the four-lane highway is a marked contrast to The President's Highway you are leaving.

The coastline is beautiful along the way, with sea and surf to the left and the drop of the Santa Ynez Mountains to the right. Up each canyon are orchards and the bones of the mountains, looking like plates stacked to dry after washing.

The highway is a civilized up-and-down, reflecting an advancement in road building technique over Refugio Pass Road. The highway begins a swing inland at Gaviota State Park (26.4), where there is a concession stand, an entrance fee, and overnight camping. Half a mile ahead is a rest stop (26.9) with restroom facilities.

The road continues through Gaviota Pass, which narrows at one point to such a defile that a tunnel through the hill takes northbound traffic, including bicyclists. The tunnel is spooky, but there is a sidewalk. Stay on Highway 101 through the Gaviota and Nojoqui passes. At the top of Nojoqui Pass, turn right down Nojoqui Grade Road (31.1), which is the old highway.

A quick downhill on the narrow, rough surface road and turn right at the bottom on the road to Nojoqui Falls Park and Solvang, Alisal Road (31.9). Across the valley, the road climbs a small hill and passes Nojoqui Falls Park (32.8). This delightful ride through an upland valley bordering the mountains turns downhill for a pleasant sweep through Alisal Canyon. As it nears the bottom the road passes Alisal Ranch resort with rodeo grounds and golf course.

Pedal across the Santa Ynez River (38.2) and up the bluff into Solvang. At the signal on Mission Drive, turn left (39.1) to the park (39.2).

stream that crosses and recrosses the road. This is not a downhill to sit back and enjoy, but rather one to watch for hazards. The road grows narrow and seems to have been paved over roots of trees and granite boulders. At last it grows somewhat flatter and more civilized and avocado and lemon groves crowd along the side of the road.

As the canyon opens to the sea, Highway 101 looms ahead. Under the

45 EAST CAMINO CIELO—THE SKY ROAD

Distance: *29 miles*
Loop
Traffic: *light to moderately heavy*
Rating: *very difficult*

I would recommend this route only to expert riders. There are several aspects that make it a stiff challenge. One is San Marcos Pass Road, which climbs 2,000 feet in seven miles with little or no shoulder and moderate, fast-moving traffic on a winding road. Then, from the top of San Marcos Pass, it climbs another 1,800 feet in nine and a half miles on a crooked mountain road with virtually no traffic.

Now there is a reward — the view. It is stunning, to the north into Los Padres National Forest and San Rafael Wilderness, and to the south down into Santa Barbara and out across the Santa Barbara Channel to the Santa Barbara Channel Islands. Take binoculars.

The ride starts at the intersection of Highways 154 and 192 in Santa Barbara. Highway 154, the San Marcos Pass Road, branches off Highway 101 north. Highway 192 is about one mile north of the 101 Freeway. Once on the bicycle, the climb up Highway 154 is immediate, although semi-subdued with a wide two-lane road that will lull the unwary as to the rest of the ride. This is the best you will be on.

There is no break in the uphill for seven miles. After two miles the shoulder shrinks and the hills crowd in on the right, covered with chaparral. Already the view opens out on the left toward the Santa Barbara Channel Islands. Nearing the top, pedal past the West Camino Cielo turn-off on the left, and as the road widens, turn right (7.0) onto East Camino Cielo at the top of San Marcos Pass. A short steep climb pulls you up to the Cielo Store, where refreshments, including sandwiches, are available. The road moves along a ridge with live oak, scrub oak and poison oak hovering over the road. Oc-

casional views north toward the San Rafaels brighten the way. A few houses hang out into space, looking toward the blue jewel of Lake Cachuma. The road grows precipitous with occasional switchbacks. Views out to the south open across the channel to the islands. The vegetation grows sparse, the road is almost one-lane, and sometimes only a rickety fence would keep one from falling off and into the sea.

A moment of flatness along a ridgetop swings around and becomes another hill to climb. Far below on the left is the Santa Ynez River valley. A downhill and then an uphill, and each time another view, sometimes looking down on the tops of hawks and buzzards. There is an absolute quiet here, only the sound of the wind and the chittering of birds break the silence.

The top is finally reached at La Cumbre Peak lookout. The elevation is 3,985 and the mileage is 16.1. The lake below is Gibraltar Reservoir on the Santa Ynez River. The tallest peak in the jumbled mass to the north is Big Pine Mountain at 6,828. To the south the marina at Santa Barbara and the wharf are dark lines in the sparkling sea.

Now the road heads down. There is one more uphill to go, but it is not far and the mountains seem to be growing somewhat less steep. The abject fear of falling off the side of the hill and landing in the surf 3,000 feet below lessens.

Take the right, downhill Y (17.9) into Rattlesnake Canyon and begin the descent. Watch your brakes for overheating as you zip down. Watch out for rocks in the road from small slides, potholes and rough road patches. The canyon narrows and the countryside begins to take on a tame look. The houses of Santa Barbara rise to meet the plunging road. The large white building on a bluff to the right of Gibraltar Road is the Monastery of Mt. Calvary.

At the intersection with El Cielito (23.9), keep to the left following the

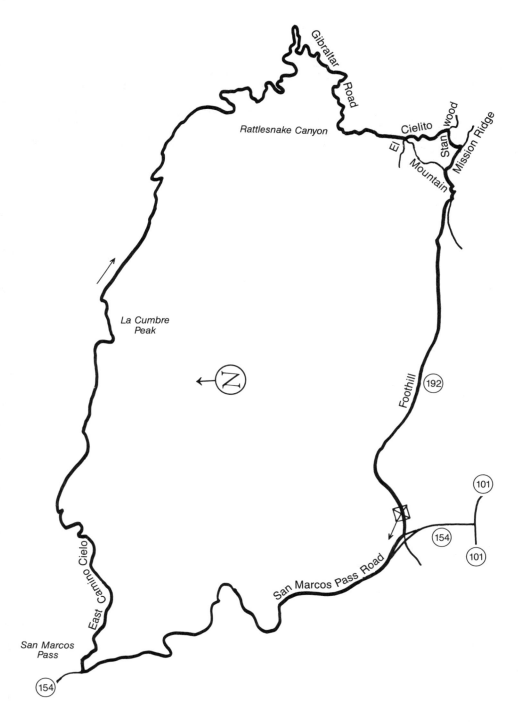

Gibraltar Road

Rattlesnake Canyon

El Cielito

Stanwood

Mission Ridge

Mountain

La Cumbre
Peak

N

Foothill

192

101

154

101

East Camino Cielo

San Marcos Pass Road

San Marcos
Pass

154

yellow stripes to the corner of Stanwood Drive (24.5), and turn right. This is Highway 192, which is the foothill highway that zooms up and down the canyons along the base of the Santa Ynez Mountains in Santa Barbara. The traffic is fairly heavy at times and there is often little or no shoulder.

Stanwood T's into Mission Ridge. Turn right. The road goes by Sheffield Reservoir and T's into Mountain Road. Go left, remaining on Highway 192, Y right onto Foothill Road (25.4) and stay on Foothill. This is an area of tennis courts and country clubs, estate homes and ups and downs. The bridge crosses San Roque Canyon, and then the road widens finally to return to the intersection with Highway 154 (29.1).

46 UNIVERSITY OF CALIFORNIA AT SANTA BARBARA

Distance: *17 miles*
Loop
Traffic: *moderate to heavy*
Rating: *easy*

The campus of the University of Santa Barbara is beautiful, rimmed on two sides by the Pacific Ocean. It is a bicycle rider's dream, with bike paths and millions of bicycles. In fact, bicycles have become the dominant mode of transportation. Riding on the campus is a look into the future if gasoline shortages are not met with new ways of fueling motorized transportation.

The ride will also include a romp through the city of Goleta and the community of Isla Vista. The area was at one

time a base for the Canalino Indians, who lived along the coastline. For years Goleta was called "The Valley of Orchids," because of orchids grown commercially, and known for citrus and walnut orchards. It is now a bedroom community for Santa Barbara and the university.

Rather arbitrarily, the ride will start at Highway 101 and Turnpike Road, which is located between Santa Barbara and Goleta.

Take Turnpike south to Hollister Avenue and turn right (0.5). Hollister is a four-lane city street with a bike lane, named for Col. W. W. Hollister, a famous California entrepreneur who made a fortune raising sheep near the town of

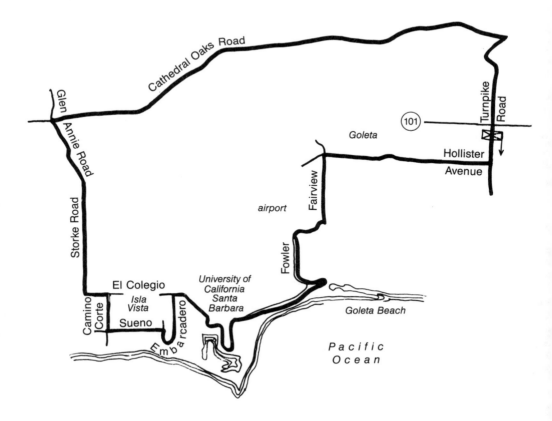

Hollister to the north and who had a ranch in Glen Annie Canyon, named for his wife. Hollister Avenue will take you through the center of Goleta's one-story-type business district.

At Fairview Avenue, turn left (2.8) through heavy traffic and pedal by the Santa Barbara Municipal Airport. Turn right onto James Fowler Road (3.5) toward the entrance to the airport. There is a bike route through here. Follow Fowler past the entrance, staying on the bike route.

Flying bicycles are liable to be passing and repassing if the university is in session. To the right is the Goleta Slough. Near the mouth of the slough, during the time of the Canalino Indians, was an island called Mescalitan where some 1,000 Canalinos lived. The slough was the home of thousands of ducks and geese and the mud flats provided clams for the Canalino menus. Dirt from the island was used to make runways for the airport and Ward Memorial Boulevard goes right over the middle of Mescalitan's location.

The bike route slips under the boulevard and by Goleta Beach County Park, where students spend their time drowsily studying in the sun and windsurfers and surfers can be watched catching the waves coming in from Goleta Point. The route pulls up away from the beach park and onto the UCSB campus (5.0).

Pick up a map of the campus from the kiosk at the East Entrance, which is off to the right as you come onto the campus. The roads are not for bicyclists — bikes have their own routes that take one throughout the middle of the campus.

There are three art galleries on campus to visit, all three open Saturday and Sunday afternoons, plus weekday hours. The University Center Cafeteria is open Mondays through Saturdays when the university is in session, although you may want to stanch your hunger in Isla Vista. The bookstore is also open Mondays through Saturdays

all day and on Sunday afternoons. The carillon at Storke Tower may be in the middle of a concert, and there are several accesses to the coastline from the campus, most south of the lagoon.

Depending on the mileage you rack up on campus you will squirt out the El Colegio Entrance on the west with something different, perhaps, but let's make it 7.5 miles, which is what I recorded.

The bike route is north of El Colegio Road, and you turn left on Embarcadero del Norte into the town of Isla Vista (7.7). There is a signal to cross El Colegio. Isla Vista is pure college town with all that implies — record shops, bare feet, bookstores, fast food, beer cellars, and people afoot. There is a tiny park, Madrid, which usually has some art work on display. From Madrid, take Sueno Road west and then turn right on Camino Corto Lane (8.9) and continue back to El Colegio. Turn left (9.2), again there is a bike route, and then right onto Storke Road (9.4).

Storke Road and Tower are named for Thomas Storke, a famous California publisher and state senator. One of Goleta's claims to fame was that during World War II the Japanese shelled the Ellwood oil fields from a submarine offshore. The occurrence was to the west of Storke Road.

Pedal past Hollister and over Highway 101. Storke Road turns into Glen Annie Road (remember Hollister's wife) and becomes rural. The heady smell of orange trees blossom the air. The road moves up toward Glen Annie Canyon, but we will make a turn right onto Cathedral Oaks Road (11.0), where a bike lane will keep us from harm. The road moves from cattle and citrus groves into a residential area. There will be some rolling ups and downs. Opposite Tucker's Grove County Park, you turn right on Turnpike Road (15.9), another road with a bike lane, and return to the start at Highway 101 (16.6).

47 HISTORY AND THE LAND—SANTA BARBARA

Distance: *10 miles*
Loop
Traffic: *moderate to heavy*
Rating: *easy to moderate*
Side trip: *12 miles, easy to moderate*

Santa Barbara has many attractions, both historical and natural. This ride will include several without ever touching the sea. The ride will visit the Santa Barbara Mission, Botanical Gardens and the Natural History Museum, with a side trip to Stow House. Take your time. The ride is not the whole thing on this journey, but rather the stops along the way.

We will start at the corner of Highways 154 and 192, San Marcos Pass and Foothill roads. The intersection can be reached by taking the San Marcos Pass off-ramp from Highway 101 and proceeding one mile north.

Begin pedaling east on Foothill, which as Highway 192 follows the base of the foothills of the Santa Ynez Mountains. On this route you will get a good look at some of the residential areas of Santa Barbara, a city of 79,200 that

grew up around the presidio, founded in 1782, and the mission, founded in 1786.

The road climbs up and down. Far above, La Cumbre Peak looks out over the city from its elevation near 4,000 feet. The road narrows, and although there is usually a shoulder, often there is not. The bridge crosses San Roque Canyon through a residential district. Turn left at the sign for the Mission Canyon Botanic Gardens onto Mission Canyon Road (3.1). The road slips up into Mission Canyon. Y right to the gardens. The parking lot (3.9) leads the way into the gardens, where native plants are grown in various areas designated as desert, canyon, island, mountain, or meadow. The gardens were established in 1926.

There are restroom facilities, a bookstore and trails up to a mile in length through the gardens. The gardens are open 8 a.m. to sunset every day. There is an admission charge. Mission Creek, the source of water for the mission when it was first built, flows through the gardens. The creek was

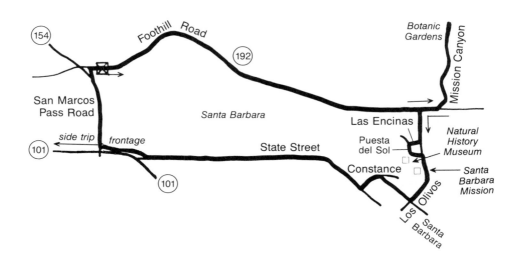

SIDE TRIP: *12.4 miles*

STOW HOUSE

Stow House is a lovely old house, the home of the first family to plant a lemon orchard in the area. The route is a pleasant one through north Goleta and involves relatively flat going. The house is open 2 to 4 p.m., Saturday and Sunday.

Crossing San Marcos Pass Road, continue on the frontage road, Calle Real, which has a bike lane. Highway 101 is to the left. Turn right on old San Marcos Road (2.0) into a development, and left on La Ramada Drive (2.3). Then a left on Ribera Drive (2.5), and right on University (2.9) to wind through this area avoiding Ygnacio Creek.

At Patterson Avenue, turn left (3.2) and pick up Calle Real again with a right turn (3.7) and pedal past a large shopping area with a bike lane. Past the shopping center the road squeezes back to two lanes, the traffic squeezes out and one has lost the city life for the country life. The road continues next to Los Carneros, a wooded, swampy area. Turn right on Los Carneros Road (6.4) and head north. Stow House is hidden off to the right just south of the Goleta Depot Railroad Museum (6.6).

The house is the headquarters for the Goleta Valley Historical Society Museum. The stately white frame farmhouse in a grove of eucalyptus was built in 1872 and the first lemon orchard was planted in 1874.

Returning to Los Carneros Road, turn right and continue up the hill to Cathedral Oaks Road (6.9). Here is a wide, peaceful street with a bike lane. At Tucker's

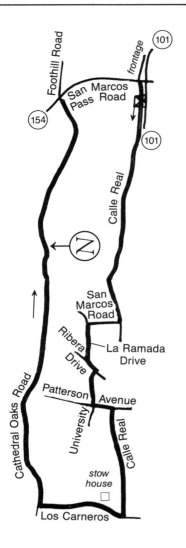

Grove County Park (10.7) there are restroom facilities and picnic tables, should a rest be in order.

Continuing on Cathedral Oaks Road there are several rolling hills and then Cathedral Oaks becomes Foothill Road at San Marcos Pass Road (12.4).

dammed in the canyon to bring a steady supply of water during the dry time of year, or during dry years.

Returning to Mission Canyon Road, speed down the canyon to Foothill and turn right (4.7) and then left on Mission Canyon Road again (4.9). At Las Encinas, turn right (5.2) to the Museum of Natural History. Follow the signs, turning left on Puesta del Sol to the museum. There is a bike rack to the right of the main entrance.

The museum is open weekdays 9 a.m. to 5 p.m. and Sundays and holidays 1 p.m. to 5 p.m., with summer Sunday and holiday hours 10 a.m. to 5 p.m. The building and grounds include displays on birds, mammals, insects, marine life, minerals, Indians, astronomy, paleontology and geology. The museum was founded in 1916. There are 11 acres on the grounds and Mission Creek tumbles through behind the buildings. There are a bookstore and an extensive library.

Continue on Puesta del Sol to the east, back to Mission Canyon Road, turn right and glide downhill to Old Mission Santa Barbara (5.8). The familiar edifice is said to be one of the most beautiful of the California missions. Tours are 9 a.m. to 5 p.m. weekdays and Saturdays, and 1 to 5 p.m. Sundays. The Moorish fountain in front was built in 1808 and was once used to wash clothes. There are many displays in the Mission museum, and the grounds are beautiful.

Leaping back on the bicycle, leave the grounds and turn right on Los Olivos Street and right on Santa Barbara Street (6.0). At Constance, turn left (6.4), as you continue through a lovely area of old Santa Barbara. Turn right onto State Street (6.6), which is a four-lane city street with heavy traffic. Even in heavy traffic, Santa Barbara is a good bicycling area because there are so

many bicyclists that motorists are used to watching for them.

At the turn toward San Marcos Pass, turn right (8.4) along the frontage road. Turn right onto Highway 154 (8.9) to complete the trip (9.7), or continue west along the frontage road for a side trip to Stow House.

48 SANTA BARBARA-BY-THE-SEA

Distance: *17 miles*
Loop
Traffic: *moderate to heavy*
Rating: *easy to moderate*

Santa Barbara is one of the most attractive cities in the Central Coast area. Situated on a bench caught between the Santa Ynez Mountains and the Pacific Ocean, the city includes exclusive residential areas, a lovely seashore, a yacht harbor and extensive shopping centers.

This trip will send the bicyclist through or by all of the above. The starting place will be at Highway 101 and the La Cumbre-Las Palmas exit into Hope Ranch.

Take the exit south onto Las Palmas Drive, which leads into Hope Ranch. The "ranch" is a beautiful development with ties that go back to 1843, when 3,282 acres were designated a Mexican land grant under the name Las Positas y Calera and given to Narciso Fabrigat. The mate on the ship in *Two Years Before the Mast* owned the area for a short time. Later, rancher Thomas Hope owned the rolling hills. The Southern Pacific Railroad Company developed the "park" as a subdivision for fine homes.

Las Palmas Drive slips by Laguna Blanca and the golf course of La Cumbre Country Club. The winding road passes riding stables and goes down a narrow canyon thick with old oaks. Las Palmas turns left onto Roble Drive and then Roble Drive turns right onto Marina Drive (2.5), lined with palm trees and estate homes.

At the "T" turn right onto Cliff Drive (3.5), which speeds downhill to Arroyo Burro Beach Park, where Arroyo Burro Creek empties into the sea. A climb brings the bicyclist up onto a bluff above the sea, and through a business district. Turn right on Meigs (5.6) and swing by La Mesa Park to turn left onto Shoreline Drive. The drive parallels the shore on the bluffs past Shoreline Park, Santa

Barbara Point, Leadbetter Beach and turns into Cabrillo Boulevard as it passes Santa Barbara City College on the left and La Playa Stadium.

Stop if you would like at the wharf and Santa Barbara Harbor to enjoy the boats and the breakwater (7.6). Continuing along Cabrillo, note the bike path along the seawalk past Stearns Wharf at Cabrillo Beach. This area, on Sunday, sports crafts and art paintings. The beach is the familiar one seen in post cards from Santa Barbara, with stately

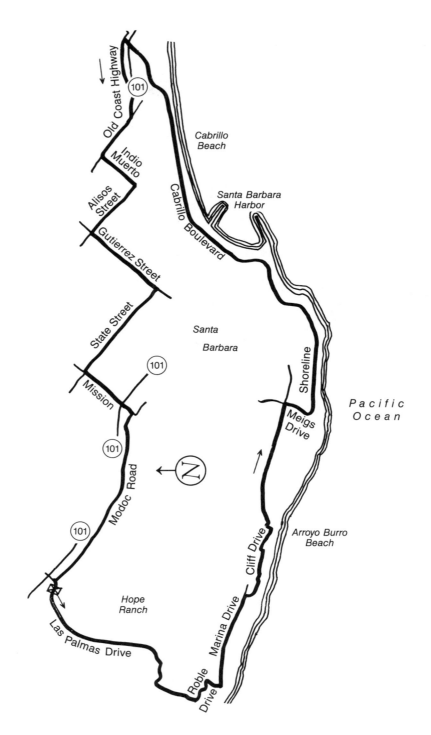

Old Coast Highway

101

Indio Muerto

Alisos Street

Gutierrez Street

State Street

Mission

101

101

101

Modoc Road

Las Palmas Drive

Hope Ranch

Roble Drive

Marina Drive

Cliff Drive

Cabrillo Beach

Cabrillo Boulevard

Santa Barbara Harbor

Santa Barbara

Shoreline

Meigs Drive

Pacific Ocean

Arroyo Burro Beach

N

palms, white sands and calm blue ocean.

The bike route switches over to the left side of Cabrillo near the Andree Clark Bird Refuge. At the northeast end of the bird refuge the ducks and geese will be only too happy to consume any leftover sandwiches you might want to offer. In fact, they are voracious enough to consume the bicycle.

Go under the freeway (10.3). Make an abrupt left turn onto Old Coast Highway and pedal along the bike lane past the Montecito County Club's beautifully green golf course, the grand old clubhouse looking down on the scene below.

Turn right on Salinas Street (11.4), go one block and turn left on Indio Muerto, which sweeps right to become Alisos Street. At Gutierrez Street, turn left, proceed to State Street and turn right. State is the festive main street of Santa Barbara with a marked bike lane. At De la Guerra and Canon Perdido streets, to the right two blocks, is the Santa Bar-

bara Presidio Historical Area. De la Guerra Plaza, City Hall, the historical museum and the beautiful County Courthouse (at Figueroa and Anacapa) are all worth seeing. Back on State Street, the Santa Barbara Museum of Art is on the right, and is open from 11 a.m. to 5 p.m. weekdays and noon to 5 p.m. on Sundays. State Street gave up being four-lane to accommodate bicycles and is a delight to pedal for a busy city street.

Turn left on Mission Street (14.6), which is difficult to bicycle, being a narrow four-lane road with heavy traffic. Only half a mile, however, will slip the bicyclist under the 101 Freeway. Turn right at the first stop sign, Modoc Road (15.2), to send one back toward the starting point. Modoc is a wide two-lane road with a bike lane that runs through a residential area, past La Cumbre Junior High School and beside the railroad tracks to the intersection with Las Palmas (17.3).

49 MONTECITO TO CARPINTERIA

Distance: *22 miles*
Loop
Traffic: *moderate*
Rating: *easy to moderate*

Two very different cities—one highly exclusive, the other seashore trendy—connected by an east-west coastline and a long sea comber, are the focus of this pleasant ride rarely out of the sight of the sea and never out of its influence. Montecito is money and country clubs and stately eucalyptus trees. Carpinteria is the sea and little houses and a one-story downtown. Each has its appeal, but the appeal is so different.

Our route will start just off Highway 101 in Montecito, at the Hot Springs Road exit. Head east along Coast Village Road through an area of quietly elegant shops. Montecito was the original choice for the site of the mission that become Old Mission Santa Barbara. It was the location of a beautiful oak forest, and even now, one thinks of trees and shade when one thinks of Montecito. It was also the site of lots of bears, grizzly bears. Now it houses Mercedes and Cadillacs. At the end of Coast Village Road, jog left and then right onto North Jamison Lane (0.7), which parallels the freeway behind an oleander hedge. On the left, shrubbery hides estates. The lane becomes Ortega Hill Road at Sheffield (2.3). Pump up the short, steep incline that separates the Montecito and Carpinteria valleys, and then scoot down through the eucalyptus trees into Summerland.

Summerland was the home of a spiritualist colony for many years and was first developed with 25-by-60 foot lots so that the spiritualists could erect tents rather than houses. The colony named the settlement Summerland, the name of the first of seven heavens in its dogma. However, there were many in the area who called Summerland "Spookville," for the spiritualists conjured up many a ghost. The biggest ghost, however, was oil. The first oil to be drilled from under the ocean came from off Summerland's shore.

Ortega Hill Road becomes Lillie and then Via Real. The road wanders along in a level way, moving out of Summerland and along the bench that drops out of the Santa Ynez Mountains. Lemons, polo grounds, quiet farm houses, pumpkins, green houses, and then, coming into Carpinteria, busier traffic.

Turn right on Santa Ynez Avenue (7.6), cross over Highway 101, and angle left onto Seventh Street toward the beach (7.8). This route is through a residential district of smaller, older homes under tall palm trees. At Linden Avenue, turn right (8.2) onto a bike lane to Carpinteria State Beach park (8.5). There is a sheltered grassy area behind the shoreline dunes with picnic tables and camping facilities.

Carpinteria was settled by the Yankees after 1850. The Carpinteria Valley was one of the few unsettled areas not a part of a Mexican land grant, and thus open for farming. Its name comes from the Spanish for carpenter shop, a name picked up from the early explorers who saw Canalino Indians making their seagoing canoes here.

Returning north on Linden Avenue, turn right on Sixth Street, go one block and turn left on Maple. The Carpinteria Valley Museum of History is on the right and is open Tuesday through Sunday, 1:30 to 4 p.m. Continue north on Maple and turn right on Carpinteria Avenue (9.0) to the historical landmark (9.6), which tells that the Chumash Indian village of Mishopshnow was discovered by Juan Rodrigues Cabrillo in 1542 and named La Carpinteria by the soldiers of the Portola Expedition in 1769.

The town was founded as a Yankee settlement in 1860 and not incorporated for one hundred years. The population is about 12,400.

Returning on Carpinteria Avenue,

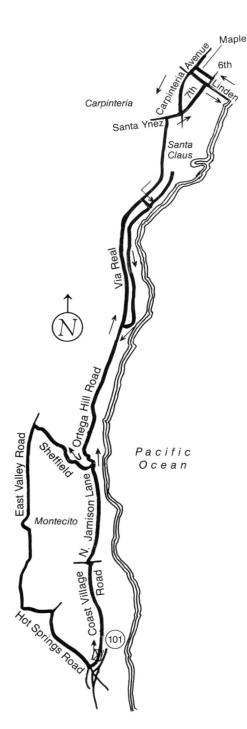

following the Pacific Coast Bicentennial Route signs, turn right on Santa Ynez Avenue and cross over the freeway (10.5). Turn left onto Via Real (10.7). At the intersection with Padaro Lane and Santa Claus Lane, turn left under the freeway (12.3). A ride into the little tourist town of Santa Claus, which has seen better days, is to the left (12.9). It has been withering away since the freeway went through without giving good ingress or egress. Returning along Padaro Lane, continue west on a narrow road with beach houses on the left, overhung with eucalyptus and cypress.

Go up and over the freeway and turn left onto Via Real (15.4). You may be bucking a headwind in the afternoon, but although bicyclists do not care for wind, the birds love it, doing their balancing act on the wind currents overhead. Pedal through Summerland, past the Big Yellow House and up Ortega Hill Road (16.7) and down to Sheffield Drive. For a tour of Montecito, turn right onto Sheffield (17.2) and pull up a gentle grade along a tree-shaded road leading past huge homes, riding stables, the Birnam Wood Golf Course, and the Valley Club of Montecito Golf Course.

At the stop sign turn left on East Valley Road (18.4). There is a narrow painted shoulder, and moderately heavy traffic. It is not comfortable bicycling. The road roller coasters through an area of estate ranches hidden behind and under trees. At San Ysidro there is a shopping mall with restaurants and a delicatessen.

Turn left just past Our Lady of Mount Carmel Church at Hot Springs Road (20.9)—there is no sign—and head down a bike lane. The road Y's right through a park-like setting, and empties out at 101 and the start of the ride (22.2).

50 CASITAS PASS AND OJAI

Distance: *46 miles*
Loop
Traffic: *light to heavy*
Rating: *difficult*

Casitas Pass to Ojai involves a climb into the Coast Range, a lake, a visit to the town of Ojai in the Ojai Valley, which was the setting for the 1940s classic movie, *Shangri-La*, a romp into the outskirts of Ventura to see the mission, and then up the coast to Carpinteria. The ride includes just about everything.

The route starts just south of Carpinteria where Highways 101 and 150 meet. Take Highway 150, the Rincon Road, northeast through a valley crowded with citrus groves. The traffic is light and there is little or no shoulder. The valley begins to move upward with precipitous farming occurring on the slopes. Trees polka-dot the sides of the hills. There is a two-and-a-half-mile uphill climb and then a downhill on a good road surface into the bottom of a narrow canyon with oaks and chaparral. Another uphill of about a mile is topped with views of Casitas Lake. Ahead on the horizon are the Topatopa Mountains with the highest peak at 6,700 feet.

The road works up and down at the edge of the lake. As the road nears the entrance the country opens out into a valley. To go to the lake, turn right at Santa Ana Road (13.3). The park at the lake includes a store, picnic area, camping facilities (the fee is $2 per night per person in the Hike and Bike section), plus, of course, fishing and hiking. It is possible to continue south on Santa Ana Road, which comes out on Highway 33, several miles south of Ojai, if you wish to miss Shangri-La. However, we will speed on to Ojai.

Following Highway 150, the valley continues to widen out as the road moves up and down through ranch lands and wooded areas, finally dropping to the Ventura River (15.3). The river is often dry with its water stored behind Matilija Dam upriver. The road is wide with a good shoulder.

To go into Ojai, turn left on the bike path just before coming to Ventura Avenue, which is Highway 33 (16.6). You will be picking up a nine-mile-long bike path between Ojai and Foster Park to the south. It is sited on a railroad right-of-way. At Libbey Park (you'll see tennis courts on your left), stash your bicycle for some foot travel.

Ojai, a city of about 8,000, has been a resort town since the 1870s, when Charles Nordhoff, of *Mutiny on the Bounty* fame, wrote about the area in Eastern newspapers. The word Ojai is Chumash and means, it is believed, "the nest." It has become a center for the arts and music. It is also the headquarters for the Theosophists. Krotona Institute has the largest library on the occult in the world. The institute is located north on Besant Road, which is on the right as you head toward Ventura. Another place worth visiting is the Ojai Valley Historical Society and Museum, on South Montgomery Street, at the end of the arcade and to the right. The museum has a particularly good exhibit of Chumash Indian artifacts, and an extensive collection of animals, snakes, birds and bird eggs from the Palmer Beaudette Foundation. It is open from 1 to 4 p.m. except Tuesdays. There are numerous restaurants in town for lunching, and motels, should you be planning an overnight.

Retrace your route out of Ojai, following the bike path to Foster Park. Ride through the park and turn left on Casitas Vista Road (27.6). This road is where the direct route from Casitas Lake via Santa Ana Road comes in. Go under the freeway and turn right onto Ventura Avenue, which will meander back and forth under the traffic on several occasions. The air is rich with the smell of lemons. As you progress south into Ventura, the Ventura Oil

Field begins to dominate the landscape and the nosescape.

The area becomes industrial in character. At West Main (33.0), turn left for a short visit to San Buenaventura Mission. The mission is on the left (33.2). It was founded on Easter Sunday, 1782, and is the ninth of the 21 California missions. If you have time, it and the surrounding grounds are well worth a visit.

To return to Carpinteria and the starting point, pedal back along West Main past Ventura Avenue. You will connect with the Pacific Coast Bicentennial Route. The route goes under the 33 Freeway, crosses the Ventura River, then slides under the 101 Freeway (34.3) on the way to Emma Wood State Beach. It follows a bike path and then joins Old State Highway. The route is along the sea and the roar of the surf will block out the roar of the traffic above. There are a number of beaches and parks along the way. The route comes up onto 101 at Sea Cliff (43.1). Exit the freeway at Bates Road (45.8) and then back up onto it again as you will have to get off and on at every exit. Keeps it interesting.

The exit off 101 to Casitas Pass, Highway 150, is the end of the route (46.4).

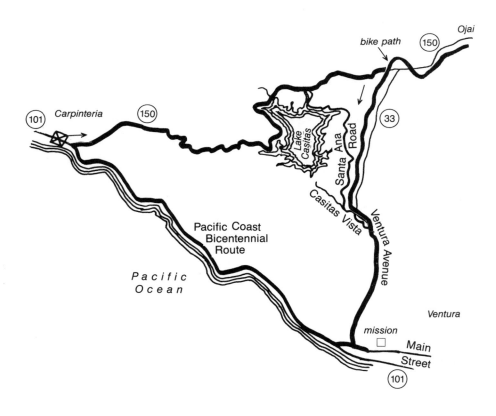